INTENT

# Prometheus's Literary Classics Series

# OSCAR WILDE

# INTENTIONS

■

## LITERARY CLASSICS

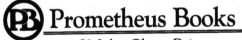 Prometheus Books

59 John Glenn Drive
Amherst, New York 14228-2197

Published 2004 by Prometheus Books

Inquiries should be addressed to
Prometheus Books
59 John Glenn Drive
Amherst, New York 14228–2197

VOICE: 716–691–0133, EXT. 207; FAX: 716–564–2711.

08 07 06 05 04     5 4 3 2 1

Library of Congress Cataloging-in-Publication Data

Wilde, Oscar, 1854–1900.
    Intentions / Oscar Wilde.
        p. cm. — (Literary classics)
    Originally published: New York : Brentano's, 1905.
    Contents: The decay of lying — Pen, pencil, and poison — The critic
as artist — The truth of masks.
    ISBN 1–59102–195–2 (alk. paper)
    1. Authorship. 2. Wainewright, Thomas Griffiths, 1794–1847.
3. Authors, English—19th century—Biography. 4. Art critics—Great
Britain—Biography. 5. Poisoners—Great Britain—Biography. I. Title.
II. Literary classics (Amherst, N.Y.)

PR5818.I7 2004
824'.8—dc22

                                                    2004044632
                                                    CIP

Printed in the United States of America on acid-free paper.

OSCAR FINGAL O'FLAHERTIE WILLS WILDE was born in Dublin, Ireland, on October 16, 1854. His father, Sir William Wilde, was a surgeon, who also published books on archaeology, folklore, and the satirist Jonathan Swift. His mother, Lady Jane Francesca Wilde, was a revolutionary poet and an authority on Celtic myth and folklore.

After attending Portora Royal School in Enniskillen, in Northern Ireland, from 1864–1871, Wilde went to Trinity College in Dublin and Magdalen College in Oxford, the latter awarding him a degree with honors. While at Magdalen College, Wilde distinguished himself not only as a classical scholar but also as a poet by winning the coveted Newdigate Prize in 1878 with the poem *Ravenna.*

In the early 1880s, when aestheticism, or art for art's sake, was the rage of literary circles in London, Wilde established himself with his flamboyance and incredible wit. Eager for acclaim, Wilde agreed to lecture in the United States and Canada in 1882, announcing on his arrival in New York City that he had "nothing to declare but his genius." Wilde urged the Americans to love beauty and art, and a year later he returned to Great Britain to lecture on his experience and his impressions of America.

Wilde married Constance Lloyd in 1884. The couple had two children, Cyril and Vyvyan, in 1885 and 1886. Wilde worked as a reviewer for the *Pall Mall Gazette* and then became editor of *Woman's World* (1887–1889). During this period he published *The Happy Prince and Other Tales* (1888).

Wilde wrote and published almost all of his major work in the last decade of his life. In his only novel, *The Picture of Dorian Gray* (published in *Lippincott's Magazine*, 1890), Wilde depicted society's fascination with youth and beauty. When critics charged that the book was scandalous and immoral, despite the title character's eventual self-destruction, Wilde revised his work, adding a preface and six chapters, and had it published in book form in 1891. *Intentions*, also published in 1891, consisting of previously published essays, further reveals the author's aesthetic attitude toward art. In the same year, he also published two volumes of stories and fairy tales, *Lord Arthur Savile's Crime, and Other Stories* and *A House of Pomegranates*, testifying to the extent of Wilde's extraordinary creative genius.

With a string of highly successful plays, including *Lady Winder-*

*mere's Fan* (1892), *Salome* (1892), *A Woman of No Importance* (1893), and *An Ideal Husband* (1895), Wilde burst onto the literary scene in the middle of the decade. His last play, *The Importance of Being Earnest* (1895), is considered his greatest.

In many of Wilde's works, the plot revolves around the exposure of a character's secret sin or indiscretion and the disgrace that this ultimately causes. If life imitates art, Wilde was himself modeling one of his characters in his reckless pursuit of pleasure. His close friendship with Lord Alfred Douglas, whom he had met in 1891, infuriated Douglas's father, the Marquess of Queensberry. When the marquess accused Wilde of sodomy, Wilde, never one to back down from a fight, sued for criminal libel. Wilde's case collapsed, however, when the evidence turned against him, and he had to drop the suit. Although his friends urged him to flee to France, Wilde refused and was arrested. After a sensational trial, he was sentenced, in May 1895, to two years' hard labor for homosexual practices. Most of his sentence was served at Reading Gaol, where he wrote a long letter to Lord Douglas, published in a shortened form in 1905 as *De Profundis*.

In May 1897 Wilde was released from prison, bankrupt, and immediately went to France, hoping to regenerate his career as a writer. He only produced one more work, *The Ballad of Reading Gaol* (1898), which expressed his concern for inhumane prison conditions. Wilde died suddenly of acute meningitis brought on by an ear infection, on November 30, 1900, in Paris.

# INTENTIONS

# CONTENTS

# INTRODUCTION

PARADOX is never so absolutely king as when you try to determine the separate ways of life and of literature. The poet lives his life, you say, and that is one matter; the poem lives its life, and that is quite another matter. Between the writer and his writings the discriminating must observe divorce. . . . Then, directly contradicting, is the theory of the goodly who are touched with the taint of Puritanism. Every written line, these hold, is the intimate expression of self. The sinner cannot write other than sinful things.

The farther you fare, if you would reach dogma on this point, the deeper will you mire. Paradox alone rules. And rules nowhere so supremely as in the case of Oscar Wilde. If, on the one hand, we plead that it is the man's letters, not his life, that posterity should cherish; on the other, it is folly for us to forget how completely, in Wilde, the artist

chose life as well as letters for expressing self.
" Life itself is an art, and has its modes of style no
less than the arts that seek to express it," wrote
Wilde in his marvellous essay on Wainewright—
marvellous in itself, and more so for the tragic
thaumaturgy by which Time made of it a prophecy
of Wilde's own fate!—and Charles Whibley, later,
echoed with " there is an art of life, as there are arts
of colour, form, and speech."   Yet, if we incline to
consider Wilde as the artist in life, if we recall
his career as æsthete, as triumphant dandy, as
successful playwright, we have also to remember
the tragedy, the prison, the dismal, horrid crum-
bling to a sordid death.   Inextricably mingled are
his living and his writing; yet to consider his
prose, his plays, his poetry, only by the light of
his prison and its aftermath, were as stupid as to
imagine that one may ever quite read any page of
his without finding there some echo of a personality.
No man whose energy, whose delight in a personal
pose, and whose paradoxic infatuation with art
could make such an impress on the time and the
land he lived in can be erased by any act of his
own, or by our volition, from the world's chronicle.
If his triumphs were gorgeous; if he turned the fogs
of London into rose-gardens for his fancy; if in
vanity and impertinence he had ruled his world as

a monarch, dictating in taste and thought and language, he was to taste, later, the depths of despair, and pain; his soul, once so arrogant in its scorn of human emotion, was to suffer sorrow, and shame and contempt. The mood of the triumphant dandy we have in his earlier, that of the self-pitying sufferer, in his later writings. In life, as in letters, he was always the man of his mood, the artist in attitudes. One must take him, if one can, at the particular mood that best pleases one.

While it is my mind now to concern myself only with that mood of Wilde's in which he produced the essays in *Intentions*, it was scarce possible to come to this without touching, however lightly, upon the perplexing, paradoxic problem of the man's life and its bearing on his art. Just as all his living was a paradox, so the relation between that living and his writing must ever remain one. A month after Wilde's death, when Puritan ears were to all intents closed against his name, I published an argument seeking to disestablish the connection between his noble artistic achievement and the cloud under which his name still lay. That was, of course, special pleading. Now, barely five years later, Time has nobly fulfilled all I then forecast. It takes no courage now, as then, upon the news of his death, to admit one's appreciation of

Oscar Wilde's artistic accomplishment. In continental Europe no play is more frequently performed at this writing than Wilde's *Salome ;* his books and his plays are everywhere conspicuous. Colder critical perspective of Time and Comparison has not diminished the regard for his writings. The posthumous publication of certain prison letters of his called *De Profundis* tended, but the other day, to darken counsel somewhat. Here, again, was the gaping wound laid open, the tortured soul writhing to find itself amid its countless attitudes. Here what had been arrogance was turned to pity, and to a pagan, yet piteous, interpretation of the Christ; yet here, still, was the pose, the attitude, the unquenchable artist in attitudes.

Nothing, in the case before us, can be thrown away. It is as futile to consider the life alone as the letters alone. All was of a piece. Yet the happy mean, the discriminating way, is, having in mind the art his life assumed, to consider as distinctly as possible the art he put on paper. His life was as complete a work of art, with heights and depths, triumphs and tragedies, as was ever composed. There, then, is one Magnum Opus. Some will like it, some loathe it; some, in reading his written art, will like to forget his acted art, some will recall it gladly: you see, do what one will, one proceeds in circles, issuing always upon paradox.

Paradox and moods, it is always these in the case of Wilde. And never more so than in the case of his essays. His fairy tales, his poetry, notably *The Ballad of Reading Gaol*, his exquisite plays—living still not only in themselves, but as models to later playwrights—have my full meed of appreciation, yet it is in his essays that I find him at his best. Here the wisdom under his paradox is most discoverable. Here, forgetting his life, one may most clearly discern his most characteristic attitude toward life. Here, in *Intentions*, are the most precious utterances of this amateur in art and life. Jewels of wit and paradox are in these pages scattered so profusely, that if once one start to pick them up, one may not stop, save for sheer weariness. Truly one may declare, as William Watson does of Lowell, that the brilliance " is so great and so ubiquitous that it pays the not inconsiderable penalty of diverting our attention from the real soundness that underlies it all. So dazzling is the flash, and at times so sharp the report, that we scarcely notice the straightness of the aim."

In that portion of the bookish world about us that fashions its verdicts upon academic formula the existence of any essayists save Lamb, Montaigne,

and Stevenson is slurred.  Yet of essayists who have
done memorable things, critically, in our own time,
there are at least three: Oscar Wilde, Bernard Shaw,
and George Moore.   All have said trenchant things
memorably.  Often impertinent, yet never negli-
gible.  *Intentions* is magnificent with impertinences,
but also with truths.   As a book, it has splendidly
the sincerity of Wilde's insincerity.   It constantly
makes ridiculous the petty formulas of petty dog-
matists.   Observe  Richard  Burton,  not  of  *New
Arabian Nights*, but of New England, declaring that
" in the  essay  an  author  stands  self-revealed;  he
may mask behind some other forms, in some measure; but commonplaceness, vulgarity, thinness of
nature, are in this kind instantly uncovered.   The
essay is for this reason a severe test."   In the very
first essay in *Intentions*, the one entitled *The Decay
of Lying*, Wilde sets all awry that assertion about
the mask and what it hides; he declares that what
is interesting about people " is the mask that each
one of them wears, not the reality that lies behind
the mask."   How, before the nimbleness of this
creature of masks and moods, can we for any length
of time observe the stolid solemnity of the dogma-
tists and the dealers in the sententious?   We are in
a land of masks and moods.

Literature is the advertisement of one's attitude

toward life. It is the record of a mood. It is the impress, writ in wax, of some mask we wore at some moment. It is a quantity of conflicting things. It is revelation, and it is masquerade. Whatever it is, literature is something of which the essays in *Intentions* must ever be accounted types: irritating, insincere, paradoxic, but—indubitably literature. Epigram jostles contradiction; truth elbows the fantastic; paradox plays through every interval; yet these essays remain arrestingly entertaining, eminently readable. Upon the style of *Intentions* there is little need to dwell; brilliant, inconsequent, mannered, it is ever the essence of the man himself. This style was the man; you can, if you will, read him in every line of it. Here are all the triumphant moods of his triumphant, arrogant years, expressed in glittering epigram and luminous diction; just as in the style of *The Ballad of Reading Gaol* you may mark the prison bars, and in that of *De Profundis* you may hear the cry of a soul desperately attempting to achieve sincerity through a chastened body.

Every one of the essays in *Intentions* marks a happy pose. The reader here has Oscar Wilde in his gayest moods. There are, in this book, four essays, the chief of them, *The Critic as Artist*, being in two parts. Every page of them is readable. You may suffer irritation, your dearest beliefs may suffer; but you will read on. This is mannered matter, from a mannered man. But man and matter hold you to the end. The author's panoply of paradox guards him against the commonplace. Never is the reader safe in assuming that the brilliant manner has nothing behind it. Let me instance the much-discussed theory about art imitating life, so adroitly set forth in the first of these essays, entitled *The Decay of Lying*. Wilde's whim, you will find, insisted upon the imitations that life gave of artistic inventions; he told of English feminine beauty actually taking on the lines and hues first created by certain painters; he told of a woman who acted exactly upon the Becky Sharp model; he gave instance upon instance. Our newspapers and our observation continually confirm the theory, at first so seemingly far-fetched. Sir Walter Besant, in his volume called *The Doubts of Dives* gave a trenchant instance in this sort of imitation. The American journalist, Julian Ralph, once recounted the incident of a model in a New York art school who absolutely, yet unconsciously, rehearsed the action of Du Maurier's heroine in suddenly refusing to pose for the altogether. Finally, do you recall the incident of Wilde's appearing before the curtain of a theatre where a play of his was being produced for the first time, and astonishing the audience with a cigarette

in his fingers, a green carnation in his lapel? Mr.
Robert Hichens afterwards used the green carnation
as the name of a satiric novelette, aimed at Wilde,
and in the spring of this year in which I write, 1905,
—nearly a score of years later, in other words,—a
florist of Los Angeles, in California, succeeded in
producing from the soil a green carnation. Who,
after that, can quite laugh out of countenance such
a sentence as this, from *The Decay of Lying*: " A
great artist invents a type, and Life tries to copy it,
to reproduce it in popular form, like an enterprising
publisher "?

The temptation to quote is hardly countered as
one reads and rereads these essays. Even before
we approach Wilde's lucid and yet elusive interpretation of the function of criticism, as expressed in
*The Critic as Artist*, we find in the earlier essay, *The
Decay of Lying*, much that bears upon this matter.
Indeed, the effort of these pages, throughout *Intentions*, is to build up the high estimate the world
should give to criticism. Always, under paradox
and contradiction, is the plea for the critic whose
art is also creative. In *The Decay of Lying* Wilde
declares that "the only portraits in which one
believes are portraits where there is very little of
the sitter and a great deal of the artist," and one has
only to think of Whistler and Sargent to realise the
germ of truth that lies here.

It is in *The Critic as Artist* that we have Wilde
at his best as brilliant essayist, keen, critical analyst.
Excepting certain impudent but amusing passages
in *The Confessions of a Young Man*, no phrases upon
contemporaries are so memorable as some that Wilde
here sets down.  Mr. Henry James, we are here told,
" writes fiction as if it were a painful duty "; Mr.
Hall Caine writes " at the top of his voice."  Of
Meredith he declared that "his style is chaos illumined
by lightning. . . . . As an artist he is everything except articulate."  Browning he termed " the most
supreme writer of fiction, it may be, that we have
ever had. . . .  The only man that can touch the hem
of his garment is George Meredith.  Meredith is a
prose Browning, and so is Browning."  He held that
" from the point of view of literature Mr. Kipling is
a genius who drops his aspirates."  For realism he
had no phrase harsh enough; he deplored novels
with a purpose, despised Zola, admired Balzac; and
summed up his theory of literature by declaring that
it meant " distinction, charm, beauty, and imaginative power."  I do not hesitate in saying that the
function of criticism in its relation to art and life has
never been better expressed than in this essay on
*The Critic as Artist.*

" Life itself is an art," he had written elsewhere,
yet now, in this essay still under consideration, he

says that "anybody can make history. Only a great man can write it." But he gives you, for that, and countless contradictions like it, plenty of epigrammatic excuse. Note this, and think of his later adventures in tragedy, and in pity: " The man who regards his past is a man who deserves to have no future to look forward to. When one has found expression for a mood, one has done with it."

Finally, there is the culminating fascination of the essay entitled *Pen, Pencil, and Poison*. This chapter on Thomas Griffiths Wainewright is one of the subtlest, uncanniest bits of appreciative writing in the history of letters. In every line of it one may read, recalling Wilde's subsequent career, the phrases of prophecy and unconscious self-revelation. It is as if he had, years before the event, given us a document that might serve as an apology or explanation. There is no argument that a pleader for Wilde could use that Wilde had not himself used here for Wainewright, who was an artist, poet, dilettante, forger, and poisoner. Now, when one has the later documents, the *Ballad* and the letters from prison, such passages as these, from *Pen, Pencil, and Poison*, ring doubly poignant: " The sentence now passed on him was, to a man of his culture, a form of death. . . . The permanence of personality is a very subtle metaphysical problem, and certainly the English law solves the question in an extremely rough-and-ready manner. . . . . His crimes seem to have had an important effect upon his art. They gave a strong personality to his style. One can fancy an intense personality being created out of sin. The fact of a man being a poisoner is nothing against his prose. The domestic virtues are not the true basis of art. There is no essential incongruity between crime and culture." There, in those words of Wilde's, written years before they could come to have application in his own case, is the expression of the vital truth that posterity can never blink, no matter how biassed. Had we before us nothing save the essay on Wainewright, there would be evidence enough for calling Wilde a brilliant creative critic. This is biography, this is art. What Robert Louis Stevenson did for Villon, briefly, brilliantly, Oscar Wilde has here done for Wainewright.

Space forbids that I dwell upon the main interpretation Wilde gives in *Intentions* of the theory of critical art. I must point you to those fascinating pages themselves, conscious that each line of mine has but delayed your coming to the feast itself. It is possible that this new edition of *Intentions* for which I make this introduction may reach some who have never yet read Wilde in the essay-form. To them my envy goes. They will close the book,

I think, upon the Wainewright essay. Unlike
Wainewright, Wilde issued from prison gay with
fine intentions. Brilliant still his talks, brilliant
still his plans. Plans for new plays, great ones.
All remained undone, unwritten. For him who
had said one must never return to the past, there
remained nothing but revocations from the Past.
Gradually all deserted him: friends, his own wit,
even the curiosity-seekers. He could no longer
talk, no longer write. The passing of the Paris
Exposition found him, and with it Death, with
all his sins upon him, huddled, so to speak, with
the memories of a splendid career, a ghastly dis-
aster. No death in all history seems more horrid
than this one. Beau Brummell in Calais, Verlaine
in Paris, do not surpass this tragedy.

The sunflowers, the lilies, the carnations, and the
velvet are gone, yet the satire and the caricature
they aroused remain part of our artistic treasure.
The tinsel of æstheticism is dust, yet we are even
now heirs to its gain in knowledge of the Japanese
arts. The drawings of Du Maurier and Beardsley,
the writings of Hichens, the words of Gilbert, all
testify obliquely to the power of the man whose
hell, more literally than that of any other man, was
indeed paved with Intentions.

PERCIVAL POLLARD.

*New York, July, 1905.*

# THE DECAY OF LYING

## AN OBSERVATION

¶ *A DIALOGUE. Persons:*
*Cyril and Vivian. Scene: the*
*library of a country house in*
*Nottinghamshire.*

# THE DECAY OF LYING

*Cyril (coming in through the open window from the terrace)*. My dear Vivian, don't coop yourself up all day in the library. It is a perfectly lovely afternoon. The air is exquisite. There is a mist upon the woods like the purple bloom upon a plum. Let us go and lie on the grass, and smoke cigarettes, and enjoy Nature.

*Vivian*. Enjoy Nature! I am glad to say that I have entirely lost that faculty. People tell us that Art makes us love Nature more than we loved her before; that it reveals her secrets to us; and that after a careful study of Corot and Constable we see things in her that had escaped our observation. My own experience is that the more we study Art, the less we care for Nature. What Art really reveals to us is Nature's lack of design, her curious crudities, her extraordinary monotony, her absolutely unfinished condition. Nature has good intentions, of course, but, as Aristotle once said, she cannot carry them

3

out.   When I look at a landscape I cannot help
seeing all its defects.   It is fortunate for us, however, that Nature is so imperfect, as otherwise we
should have had no art at all.   Art is our spirited
protest, our gallant attempt to teach Nature her
proper place.   As for the infinite variety of Nature,
that is a pure myth.   It is not to be found in Nature
herself.   It resides in the imagination, or fancy, or
cultivated blindness of the man who looks at her.

*Cyril.* Well, you need not look at the landscape.
You can lie on the grass and smoke and talk.

*Vivian.* But Nature is so uncomfortable.   Grass is
hard and lumpy and damp, and full of dreadful black
insects.   Why, even Morris' poorest workman could
make you a more comfortable seat than the whole of
Nature can.   Nature pales before the furniture of "the
street which from Oxford has borrowed its name," as
the poet you love so much once vilely phrased it.   I
don't complain.   If Nature had been comfortable,
mankind would never have invented architecture, and
I prefer houses to the open air.   In a house we all feel
of the proper proportions.   Everything is subordinated
to us, fashioned for our use and our pleasure.   Egotism
itself, which is so necessary to a proper sense of
human dignity, is entirely the result of indoor life.
Out of doors one becomes abstract and impersonal.
One's individuality absolutely leaves one.   And then

Nature is so indifferent, so unappreciative. Whenever I am walking in the park here, I always feel
that I am no more to her than the cattle that
browse on the slope, or the burdock that blooms in
the ditch. Nothing is more evident than that Nature
hates Mind. Thinking is the most unhealthy thing
in the world, and people die of it just as they die
of any other disease. Fortunately, in England at
any rate, thought is not catching. Our splendid
physique as a people is entirely due to our national
stupidity. I only hope we shall be able to keep
this great historic bulwark of our happiness for
many years to come; but I am afraid that we
are beginning to be over-educated; at least everybody who is incapable of learning has taken to
teaching—that is really what our enthusiasm for
education has come to. In the meantime, you had
better go back to your wearisome, uncomfortable
Nature, and leave me to correct my proofs.

*Cyril.* Writing an article! That is not very consistent after what you have just said.

*Vivian.* Who wants to be consistent? The dullard
and the doctrinaire, the tedious people who carry out
their principles to the bitter end of action, to the
*reductio ad absurdum* of practice. Not I. Like
Emerson, I write over the door of my library the
word " Whim." Besides, my article is really a most

salutary and valuable warning. If it is attended to, there may be a new Renaissance of Art.

*Cyril.* What is the subject?

*Vivian.* I intend to call it " The Decay of Lying : A Protest."

*Cyril.* Lying! I should have thought that our politicians kept up that habit.

*Vivian.* I assure you that they do not. They never rise beyond the level of misrepresentation, and actually condescend to prove, to discuss, to argue. How different from the temper of the true liar, with his frank, fearless statements, his superb responsibility, his healthy, natural disdain of proof of any kind! After all, what is a fine lie? Simply that which is its own evidence. If a man is sufficiently unimaginative to produce evidence in support of a lie, he might just as well speak the truth at once. No, the politicians won't do. Something may, perhaps, be urged on behalf of the Bar. The mantle of the Sophist has fallen on its members. Their feigned ardours and unreal rhetoric are delightful. They can make the worse appear the better cause, as though they were fresh from Leontine schools, and have been known to wrest from reluctant juries triumphant verdicts of acquittal for their clients, even when those clients, as often happens, were clearly and unmistakeably innocent. But they are briefed by the prosaic, and are not ashamed to appeal to precedent. In spite of their endeavours, the truth will out.    Newspapers, even, have degenerated.    They may now be absolutely relied upon.    One feels it as one wades through their columns.    It is always the unreadable that occurs. I am afraid that there is not much to be said in favour of either the lawyer or the journalist. Besides what I am pleading for is Lying in art.    Shall I read you what I have written?    It might do you a great deal of good.

*Cyril.* Certainly, if you give me a cigarette. Thanks.    By the way, what magazine do you intend it for?

*Vivian.* For the *Retrospective Review.*    I think I told you that the elect had revived it.

*Cyril.* Whom do you mean by " the elect "?

*Vivian.* Oh, The Tired Hedonists of course.    It is a club to which I belong.    We are supposed to wear faded roses in our button-holes when we meet, and to have a sort of cult for Domitian.    I am afraid you are not eligible.    You are too fond of simple pleasures.

*Cyril.* I should be black-balled on the ground of animal spirits, I suppose?

*Vivian.* Probably.    Besides, you are little too old. We don't admit anybody who is of the usual age.

*Cyril.* Well, I should fancy you are all a good deal bored with each other.

*Vivian.* We are.    That is one of the objects of

the club.    Now, if you promise not to interrupt too
often, I will read you my article.

*Cyril.* You will find me all attention.

*Vivian (reading in a very clear, musical voice).*
"THE DECAY OF LYING: A PROTEST.—One of
the chief causes that can be assigned for the
curiously commonplace character of most of the
literature of our age is undoubtedly the decay of
Lying as an art, a science, and a social pleasure.
The ancient historians gave us delightful fiction in
the form of fact; the modern novelist presents us
with dull facts under the guise of fiction.    The
Blue-Book is rapidly becoming his ideal both for
method and manner.    He has his tedious ' *document
humain*,' his miserable little '*coin de la création*,' into
which he peers with his microscope.    He is to be
found at the Librairie Nationale, or at the British
Museum, shamelessly reading up his subject.    He
has not even the courage of other people's ideas,
but insists on going directly to life for everything,
and ultimately, between encyclopædias and personal
experience, he comes to the ground, having
drawn his types from the family circle or from the
weekly washerwoman, and having acquired an
amount of useful information from which never,
even in his most meditative moments, can he
thoroughly free himself.

" The loss that results to literature in general from this false ideal of our time can hardly be overestimated. People have a careless way of talking about a ' born liar,' just as they talk about a ' born poet.' But in both cases they are wrong. Lying and poetry are arts—arts, as Plato saw, not unconnected with each other—and they require the most careful study, the most disinterested devotion. Indeed, they have their technique, just as the more material arts of painting and sculpture have, their subtle secrets of form and colour, their craft-mysteries, their deliberate artistic methods. As one knows the poet by his fine music, so one can recognize the liar by his rich rhythmic utterance, and in neither case will the casual inspiration of the moment suffice. Here, as elsewhere, practice must precede perfection. But in modern days while the fashion of writing poetry has become far too common, and should, if possible, be discouraged, the fashion of lying has almost fallen into disrepute. Many a young man starts in life with a natural gift for exaggeration which, if nurtured in congenial and sympathetic surroundings, or by the imitation of the best models, might grow into something really great and wonderful. But, as a rule, he comes to nothing. He either falls into careless habits of accuracy——"

*Cyril.* My dear fellow!

*Vivian.* Please don't interrupt in the middle of a sentence.  " He either falls into careless habits of accuracy, or takes to frequenting the society of the aged and the well-informed.  Both things are equally fatal to his imagination, as indeed they would be fatal to the imagination of anybody, and in a short time he develops a morbid and unhealthy faculty of truth-telling, begins to verify all statements made in his presence, has no hesitation in contradicting people who are much younger than himself, and often ends by writing novels which are so like life that no one can possibly believe in their probability.  This is no isolated instance that we are giving.  It is simply one example out of many ; and if something cannot be done to check, or at least to modify, our monstrous worship of facts, Art will become sterile and Beauty will pass away from the land.

" Even Mr. Robert Louis Stevenson, that delightful master of delicate and fanciful prose, is tainted with this modern vice, for we know positively no other name for it.  There is such a thing as robbing a story of its reality by trying to make it too true, and *The Black Arrow* is so inartistic as not to contain a single anachronism to boast of, while the transformation of Dr. Jekyll reads dangerously like an experiment out of the *Lancet*. As for Mr. Rider Haggard, who really has, or had once, the makings of a perfectly magnificent liar, he is now so afraid of being suspected of genius that when he does tell us anything marvellous, he feels bound to invent a personal reminiscence, and to put it into a footnote as a kind of cowardly corroboration. Nor are our other novelists much better. Mr. Henry James writes fiction as if it were a painful duty, and wastes upon mean motives and imperceptible 'points of view' his neat literary style, his felicitous phrases, his swift and caustic satire. Mr. Hall Caine, it is true, aims at the grandiose, but then he writes at the top of his voice. He is so loud that one cannot hear what he says. Mr. James Payn is an adept in the art of concealing what is not worth finding. He hunts down the obvious with the enthusiasm of a short-sighted detective. As one turns over the pages, the suspense of the author becomes almost unbearable. The horses of Mr. William Black's phaeton do not soar towards the sun. They merely frighten the sky at evening into violent chromolithographic effects. On seeing them approach, the peasants take refuge in dialect. Mrs. Oliphant prattles pleasantly about curates, lawn-tennis parties, domesticity, and other wearisome things. Mr. Marion Crawford has immolated himself upon the altar of local colour. He is like the lady in the French comedy who keeps talking about 'le beau ciel d'Italie.' Besides, he has fallen into a bad habit of uttering moral platitudes. He is always telling us that to be good is to be good, and that to be bad is to be wicked. At times he is almost edifying. *Robert Elsmere* is of course a masterpiece—a masterpiece of the ' genre ennuyeux,' the one form of literature that the English people seem to thoroughly enjoy. A thoughtful young friend of ours once told us that it reminded him of the sort of conversation that goes on at a meat tea in the house of a serious Noncomformist family, and we can quite believe it. Indeed it is only in England that such a book could be produced. England is the home of lost ideas. As for that great and daily increasing school of novelists for whom the sun always rises in the East-End, the only thing that can be said about them is that they find life crude, and leave it raw.

"In France, though nothing so deliberately tedious as *Robert Elsmere* has been produced, things are not much better. M. Guy de Maupassant, with his keen mordant irony and his hard vivid style, strips life of the few poor rags that still cover her, and shows us foul sore and festering wound. He writes lurid little tragedies in which everybody is ridiculous; bitter comedies at which one cannot laugh for very tears.  M. Zola, true to the lofty principle that he lays down in one of his pronunciamientos on literature, ' L'homme de génie n'a jamais d'esprit,' is determined to show that, if he has not got genius, he can at least be dull. And how well he succeeds!  He is not without power.    Indeed at times, as in *Germinal*, there is something almost epic in his work.   But his work is entirely wrong from beginning to end, and wrong not on the ground of morals, but on the ground of art. From any ethical standpoint it is just what it should be. The author is perfectly truthful, and describes things exactly as they happen.  What more can any moralist desire?  We have no sympathy at all with the moral indignation of our time against M. Zola.   It is simply the indignation of Tartuffe on being exposed. But from the standpoint of art, what can be said in favour of the author of *L'Assommoir, Nana*, and *Pot-Bouille?*  Nothing.   Mr. Ruskin once described the characters in George Eliot's novels as being like the sweepings of a Pentonville omnibus, but M. Zola's characters are much worse.   They have their dreary vices, and their drearier virtues.  The record of their lives is absolutely without interest.   Who cares what happens to them ?   In literature we require distinction, charm, beauty, and imaginative power.   We

don't want to be harrowed and disgusted with an
account of the doings of the lower orders. M. Daudet
is better.    He has wit, a light touch, and an amusing style.    But he has lately committed literary
suicide.  Nobody can possibly care for Delobelle
with his 'Il faut lutter pour l'art,' or for Valmajour
with his eternal refrain about the nightingale, or for
the poet in *Jack* with his 'mots cruels,' now that we
have learned from *Vingt Ans de ma Vie littéraire*
that these characters were taken directly from life.
To us they seem to have suddenly lost all their
vitality, all the few qualities they ever possessed.
The only real people are the people who never
existed, and if a novelist is base enough to go to life
for his personages he should at least pretend that they
are creations, and not boast of them as copies.    The
justification of a character in a novel is not that
other persons are what they are, but that the author
is what he is.    Otherwise the novel is not a work of
art.    As for M. Paul Bourget, the master of the 'roman
psychologique,' he commits the error of imagining that
the men and women of modern life are capable of
being infinitely analysed for an innumerable series of
chapters.    In point of fact what is interesting about
people in good society—and M. Bourget rarely moves
out of the Faubourg St. Germain, except to come
to London,—is the mask that each one of them

wears, not the reality that lies behind the mask. It is a humiliating confession, but we are all of us made out of the same stuff. In Falstaff there is something of Hamlet, in Hamlet there is not a little of Falstaff. The fat knight has his moods of melancholy, and the young prince his moments of coarse humour. Where we differ from each other is purely in accidentals: in dress, manner, tone of voice, religious opinions, personal appearance, tricks of habit, and the like. The more one analyses people, the more all reasons for analysis disappear. Sooner or later one comes to that dreadful universal thing called human nature. Indeed, as any one who has ever worked among the poor knows only too well, the brotherhood of man is no mere poet's dream, it is a most depressing and humiliating reality; and if a writer insists upon analysing the upper classes, he might just as well write of match-girls and costermongers at once." However, my dear Cyril, I will not detain you any further just here. I quite admit that modern novels have many good points. All I insist on is that, as a class, they are quite unreadable.

*Cyril.* That is certainly a very grave qualification, but I must say that I think you are rather unfair in some of your strictures. I like *The Deemster*, and *The Daughter of Heth*, and *Le Disciple*, and *Mr. Isaacs*, and as for *Robert Elsmere* I am quite devoted to it.

Not that I can look upon it as a serious work.   As a statement of the problems that confront the earnest Christian it is ridiculous and antiquated.   It is simply Arnold's *Literature and Dogma* with the literature left out.   It is as much behind the age as Paley's *Evidences*, or Colenso's method of Biblical exegesis. Nor could anything be less impressive than the unfortunate hero gravely heralding a dawn that rose long ago, and so completely missing its true significance that he proposes to carry on the business of the old firm under the new name.   On the other hand, it contains several clever caricatures, and a heap of delightful quotations, and Green's philosophy very pleasantly sugars the somewhat bitter pill of the author's fiction.   I also cannot help expressing my surprise that you have said nothing about the two novelists whom you are always reading, Balzac and George Meredith.   Surely they are realists, both of them?

*Vivian.* Ah!   Meredith!   Who can define him? His style is chaos illumined by flashes of lightning.   As a writer he has mastered everything except language : as a novelist he can do everything, except tell a story : as an artist he is everything, except articulate. Somebody in Shakespeare—Touchstone, I think— talks about a man who is always breaking his shins over his own wit, and it seems to me that this might serve as the basis for a criticism of Meredith's method. But whatever he is, he is not a realist. Or rather I would say that he is a child of realism who is not on speaking terms with his father. By deliberate choice he has made himself a romanticist. He has refused to bow the knee to Baal, and after all, even if the man's fine spirit did not revolt against the noisy assertions of realism, his style would be quite sufficient of itself to keep life at a respectful distance. By its means he has planted round his garden a hedge full of thorns, and red with wonderful roses. As for Balzac, he was a most wonderful combination of the artistic temperament with the scientific spirit. The latter he bequeathed to his disciples: the former was entirely his own. The difference between such a book as M. Zola's *L'Assommoir* and Balzac's *Illusions Perdues* 's the difference between unimaginative realism and imaginative reality. "All Balzac's characters," said Baudelaire, "are gifted with the same ardour of life that animated himself. All his fictions are as deeply coloured as dreams. Each mind is a weapon loaded to the muzzle with will. The very scullions have genius." A steady course of Balzac reduces our living friends to shadows, and our acquaintances to the shadows of shades. His characters have a kind of fervent fiery-coloured existence. They dominate us, and defy scepticism. One

of the greatest tragedies of my life is the death of
Lucien de Rubempré.    It is a grief from which I
have never been able to completely rid myself.    It
haunts me in my moments of pleasure.    I remember
it when I laugh.    But Balzac is no more a realist than
Holbein was.    He created life, he did not copy it.
I admit, however, that he set far too high a value on
modernity of form and that, consequently, there is
no book of his that, as an artistic masterpiece, can
rank with *Salammbô* or *Esmond*, or *The Cloister and
the Hearth*, or the *Vicomte de Bragelonne.*

*Cyril.*  Do you object to modernity of form,
then ?

*Vivian.* Yes.    It is a huge price to pay for a very
poor result.  Pure modernity of form is always somewhat vulgarising.    It cannot help being so.    The public imagine that, because they are interested in their
immediate surroundings, Art should be interested in
them also, and should take them as her subject-
matter.    But the mere fact that they are interested
in these things makes them unsuitable subjects for
Art.    The only beautiful things, as somebody once
said, are the things that do not concern us.    As long
as a thing is useful or necessary to us, or affects us in
any way, either for pain or for pleasure, or appeals
strongly to our sympathies, or is a vital part of the
environment in which we live, it is outside the proper

sphere of art.   To art's subject-matter we should be
more or less indifferent.   We should, at any rate,
have no preferences, no prejudices, no partisan feeling of any kind.   It is exactly because Hecuba is
nothing to us that her sorrows are such an admirable
motive for a tragedy.   I do not know anything in the
whole history of literature sadder than the artistic
career of Charles Reade.   He wrote one beautiful
book, *The Cloister and the Hearth*, a book as much
above *Romola* as *Romola* is above *Daniel Deronda*,
and wasted the rest of his life in a foolish attempt to
be modern, to draw public attention to the state of our
convict prisons, and the management of our private
lunatic asylums.   Charles Dickens was depressing
enough in all conscience when he tried to arouse our
sympathy for the victims of the poor-law administra-
tion; but Charles Reade, an artist, a scholar, a man
with a true sense of beauty, raging and roaring over
the abuses of contemporary life like a common pam-
phleteer or a sensational journalist, is really a sight for
the angels to weep over.   Believe me, my dear Cyril,
modernity of form and modernity of subject-matter
are entirely and absolutely wrong.   We have mistaken the common livery of the age for the vesture of
the Muses, and spend our days in the sordid streets
and hideous suburbs of our vile cities when we should
be out on the hillside with Apollo.   Certainly we are

a degraded race, and have sold our birthright for a mess of facts.

*Cyril.* There is something in what you say, and there is no doubt that whatever amusement we may find in reading a purely modern novel, we have rarely any artistic pleasure in re-reading it. And this is perhaps the best rough test of what is literature and what is not. If one cannot enjoy reading a book over and over again, there is no use reading it at all. But what do you say about the return to Life and Nature? This is the panacea that is always being recommended to us.

*Vivian.* I will read you what I say on that subject. The passage comes later on in the article, but I may as well give it to you now:—

"The popular cry of our time is 'Let us return to Life and Nature; they will recreate Art for us, and send the red blood coursing through her veins; they will shoe her feet with swiftness and make her hand strong.' But, alas! we are mistaken in our amiable and well-meaning efforts. Nature is always behind the age. And as for Life, she is the solvent that breaks up Art, the enemy that lays waste her house."

*Cyril.* What do you mean by saying that Nature is always behind the age?

*Vivian.* Well, perhaps that is rather cryptic. What

I mean is this. If we take Nature to mean natural simple instinct as opposed to self-conscious culture, the work produced under this influence is always old-fashioned, antiquated, and out of date. One touch of Nature may make the whole world kin, but two touches of Nature will destroy any work of Art. If, on the other hand, we regard Nature as the collection of phenomena external to man, people only discover in her what they bring to her. She has no suggestions of her own. Wordsworth went to the lakes, but he was never a lake poet. He found in stones the sermons he had already hidden there. He went moralizing about the district, but his good work was produced when he returned, not to Nature but to poetry. Poetry gave him *Laodamia*, and the fine sonnets, and the great Ode, such as it is. Nature gave him *Martha Ray* and *Peter Bell*, and the address to Mr. Wilkinson's spade.

*Cyril.* I think that view might be questioned. I am rather inclined to believe in the "impulse from a vernal wood," though of course the artistic value of such an impulse depends entirely on the kind of temperament that receives it, so that the return to Nature would come to mean simply the advance to a great personality. You would agree with that, I fancy. However, proceed with your article.

*Vivian (reading).* "Art begins with abstract deco-

ration with purely imaginative and pleasurable work
dealing with what is unreal and non-existent. This is
the first stage.    Then Life becomes fascinated with
this  new wonder, and asks to be admitted into the
charmed circle.    Art takes life as part of her rough
material, recreates it, and refashions it in fresh forms,
is absolutely indifferent to fact, invents, imagines,
dreams, and keeps between herself and reality the
impenetrable barrier of beautiful style, of decorative
or ideal treatment.    The third stage is when Life gets
the upper hand, and drives Art out into the wilderness.    This is the true decadence, and it is from this
that we are now suffering.

" Take the case of the English drama.    At first in
the hands of the monks Dramatic Art was abstract,
decorative, and mythological.    Then she enlisted Life
in her service, and using some of life's external forms,
she created  an entirely new race of beings, whose
sorrows were more terrible than any sorrow man has
ever felt, whose joys were keener than lover's joys,
who had  the  rage of  the Titans  and  the  calm of
the  gods,  who  had  monstrous  and  marvellous
sins, monstrous and marvellous virtues.    To them
she  gave a language different from that of actual
use, a  language full of  resonant music  and  sweet
rhythm, made stately by solemn cadence, or made
delicate by fanciful rhyme, jewelled with wonderful

words, and enriched with lofty diction.   She clothed her children in strange raiment and gave them masks, and at her bidding the antique world rose from its marble tomb.   A new Cæsar stalked through the streets of risen Rome, and with purple sail and flute-led oars another Cleopatra passed up the river to Antioch.  Old myth and legend and dream took shape and substance.   History was entirely rewritten, and there was hardly one of the dramatists who did not recognize that the object of Art is not simple truth but complex beauty.   In this they were perfectly right.   Art itself is really a form of exaggeration; and selection, which is the very spirit of art, is nothing more than an intensified mode of over-emphasis.

"But Life soon shattered the perfection of the form.   Even in Shakespeare we can see the beginning of the end.   It shows itself by the gradual breaking up of the blank-verse in the later plays, by the predominance given to prose, and by the over-importance assigned to characterisation.   The passages in Shakespeare—and they are many—where the language is uncouth, vulgar, exaggerated, fantastic, obscene even, are entirely due to Life calling for an echo of her own voice, and rejecting the intervention of beautiful style, through which alone should Life be suffered to find expression.   Shakespeare is not by any means a flawless artist.   He is too fond of going directly to life, and borrowing life's natural utterance. He forgets that when Art surrenders her imaginative medium she surrenders everything. Goethe says, somewhere—

In der Beschränkung zeigt sich erst der Meister,

'It is in working within limits that the master reveals himself,' and the limitation, the very condition of any art is style. However, we need not linger any longer over Shakespeare's realism. *The Tempest* is the most perfect of palinodes. All that we desired to point out was, that the magnificent work of the Elizabethan and Jacobean artists contained within itself the seeds of its own dissolution, and that, if it drew some of its strength from using life as rough material, it drew all its weakness from using life as an artistic method. As the inevitable result of this substitution of an imitative for a creative medium, this surrender of an imaginative form, we have the modern English melodrama. The characters in these plays talk on the stage exactly as they would talk off it; they have neither aspirations nor aspirates; they are taken directly from life and reproduce its vulgarity down to the smallest detail; they present the gait, manner, costume, and accent of real people; they would pass unnoticed in a third-class railway carriage. And yet how wearisome the plays

are ! They do not succeed in producing even that
impression of reality at which they aim, and which
is their only reason for existing.    As a method, realism is a complete failure.

" What is true about the drama and the novel is no
less true about those arts that we call the decorative
arts.    The whole history of these arts in Europe is
the record of the struggle between Orientalism,
with its frank rejection of imitation, its love of artistic convention, its dislike to the actual representa-
tion of any object in Nature, and our own imitative
spirit.    Wherever the former has been paramount,
as in Byzantium, Sicily, and Spain, by actual contact, or in the rest of Europe by the influence of
the Crusades, we have had beautiful and imaginative work in which the visible things of life are
transmuted into artistic conventions, and the things
that Life has not are invented and fashioned for her
delight.    But wherever we have returned to Life
and Nature, our work has always become vulgar,
common, and uninteresting.    Modern tapestry, with
its aërial effects, its elaborate perspective, its broad
expanses of waste sky, its faithful and laborious
realism, has no beauty whatsoever.    The pictorial
glass of Germany is absolutely detestable.    We are
beginning to weave possible carpets in England,
but only because we have returned to the method

and spirit of the East.   Our rugs and carpets of
twenty years ago, with their solemn depressing
truths, their inane worship of Nature, their sordid
reproductions of visible objects, have become, even
to the Philistine, a source of laughter.   A cultured
Mahomedan once remarked to us, 'You Christians
are so occupied in misinterpreting the fourth com-
mandment that you have never thought of making
an artistic application of the second.'   He was perfectly right, and the whole truth of the matter is
this: The proper school to learn art in is not Life
but Art."

And now let me read you a passage which seems
to me to settle the question very completely.

" It was not always thus.   We need not say anything about the poets, for they, with the unfortunate exception of Mr. Wordsworth, have been really
faithful to their high mission, and are universally
recognized as being absolutely unreliable.   But in
the works of Herodotus, who, in spite of the shallow and ungenerous attempts of modern sciolists to
verify his history, may justly be called the 'Father
of Lies'; in the published speeches of Cicero and
the biographies of Suetonius; in Tacitus at his best;
in Pliny's *Natural History;* in Hanno's *Periplus;*
in all the early chronicles; in the Lives of the
Saints; in Froissart and Sir Thomas Mallory; in

the travels of Marco Polo; in Olaus Magnus, and Aldrovandus, and Conrad Lycosthenes, with his magnificent *Prodigiorum et Ostentorum Chronicon;* in the autobiography of Benvenuto Cellini; in the memoirs of Casanuova; in Defoe's *History of the Plague;* in Boswell's *Life of Johnson;* in Napoleon's despatches, and in the works of our own Carlyle, whose *French Revolution* is one of the most fascinating historical novels ever written, facts are either kept in their proper subordinate position, or else entirely excluded on the general ground of dulness. Now, everything is changed.   Facts are not merely finding a footing-place in history, but they are usurping the domain of Fancy, and have invaded the kingdom of Romance.   Their chilling touch is over everything.   They are vulgarising mankind. The crude commercialism of America, its materialising spirit, its indifference to the poetical side of things, and its lack of imagination and of high unattainable ideals, are entirely due to that country having adopted for its national hero a man, who according to his own confession, was incapable of telling a lie, and it is not too much to say that the story of George Washington and the cherry-tree has done more harm, and in a shorter space of time, than any other moral tale in the whole of literature."

*Cyril.* My dear boy!

*Vivian.* I assure you it is the case, and the amusing part of the whole thing is that the story of the cherry-tree is an absolute myth. However, you must not think that I am too despondent about the artistic future either of America or of our own country. Listen to this:—

"That some change will take place before this century has drawn to its close we have no doubt whatsoever. Bored by the tedious and improving conversation of those who have neither the wit to exaggerate nor the genius to romance, tired of the intelligent person whose reminiscences are always based upon memory. whose statements are invariably limited by probability, and who is at any time liable to be corroborated by the merest Philistine who happens to be present, Society sooner or later must return to its lost leader, the cultured and fascinating liar. Who he was who first, without ever having gone out to the rude chase, told the wondering cavemen at sunset how he had dragged the Megatherium from the purple darkness of its jasper cave, or slain the Mammoth in single combat and brought back its gilded tusks, we cannot tell, and not one of our modern anthropologists, for all their much-boasted science, has had the ordinary courage to tell us. Whatever was his name or race, he

certainly was the true founder of social intercourse.
For the aim of the liar is simply to charm, to delight, to give pleasure.  He is the very basis of
civilized society, and without him a dinner party,
even at the mansions of the great, is as dull as a
lecture at the Royal Society, or a debate at the In-
corporated Authors, or one of Mr. Burnand's far-
cical comedies.

" Nor will he be welcomed by society alone.  Art,
breaking from the prison-house of realism, will run
to greet him, and will kiss his false, beautiful lips,
knowing that he alone is in possession of the great
secret of all her manifestations, the secret that
Truth is entirely and absolutely a matter of style;
while Life—poor, probable, uninteresting human
life—tired of repeating herself for the benefit of
Mr. Herbert Spencer, scientific historians, and the
compilers of statistics in general, will follow meekly
after him, and try to reproduce, in her own simple and
untutored way, some of the marvels of which he talks.

" No doubt there will always be critics who, like
a certain writer in the *Saturday Review*, will gravely
censure the teller of fairy tales for his defective knowledge of natural history, who will measure imaginative
work by their own lack of any imaginative faculty,
and will hold up their inkstained hands in horror
if some honest gentleman, who has never been

farther than the yew-trees of his own garden, pens
a fascinating book of travels like Sir John Mande-
ville, or, like great Raleigh, writes a whole history
of the world, without knowing anything whatsoever
about the past.   To excuse themselves they will try
and shelter under the shield of him who made Prospero the magician, and gave him Caliban and Ariel
as his servants, who heard the Tritons blowing their
horns round the coral reefs of the Enchanted Isle,
and the fairies singing to each other in a wood near
Athens, who led the phantom kings in dim proces-
sion across the misty Scottish heath, and hid Hecate
in a cave with the weird sister.   They will call
upon Shakespeare—they always do—and will quote
that hackneyed passage about Art holding the mirror up to Nature, forgetting that this unfortunate
aphorism is deliberately said by Hamlet in order to
convince the bystanders of his absolute insanity in
all art-matters."

*Cyril.* Ahem!   Another cigarette, please.

*Vivian.* My dear fellow, whatever you may say,
it is merely a dramatic utterance, and no more represents Shakespeare's real views upon art than the
speeches of Iago represent his real views upon
morals.   But let me get to the end of the passage:

"Art finds her own perfection within, and not
outside of, herself.   She is not to be judged by any

external standard of resemblance.  She is a veil, rather than a mirror.  She has flowers that no forests know of, birds that no woodland possesses. She makes and unmakes many worlds, and can draw the moon from heaven with a scarlet thread. Hers are the 'forms more real than living man,' and hers the great archetypes of which things that have existence are but unfinished copies.  Nature has, in her eyes, no laws, no uniformity.  She can work miracles at her will, and when she calls monsters from the deep they come.  She can bid the almond tree blossom in winter, and send the snow upon the ripe cornfield.  At her word the frost lays its silver finger on the burning mouth of June, and the winged lions creep out from the hollows of the Lydian hills.  The dryads peer from the thicket as she passes by, and the brown fauns smile strangely at her when she comes near them. She has hawk-faced gods that worship her, and the centaurs gallop at her side."

*Cyril.* I like that.  I can see it.  Is that the end?

*Vivian.* No.  There is one more passage, but it is purely practical.  It simply suggests some methods by which we could revive this lost art of Lying.

*Cyril.* Well, before you read it to me, I should like to ask you a question.  What do you mean by saying that life, "poor, probable, uninteresting human life," will try to reproduce the marvels of art? I can quite understand your objection to art being treated as a mirror. You think it would reduce genius to the position of a cracked looking-glass. But you don't mean to say that you seriously believe that Life imitates Art, that Life in fact is the mirror, and Art the reality?

*Vivian.* Certainly I do. Paradox though it may seem—and paradoxes are always dangerous things—it is none the less true that Life imitates art far more than Art imitates life. We have all seen in our own day in England how a certain curious and fascinating type of beauty, invented and emphasised by two imaginative painters, has so influenced Life that whenever one goes to a private view or to an artistic salon one sees, here the mystic eyes of Rossetti's dream, the long ivory throat, the strange square-cut jaw, the loosened shadowy hair that he so ardently loved, there the sweet maidenhood of *The Golden Stair*, the blossom-like mouth and weary loveliness of the *Laus Amoris*, the passion-pale face of Andromeda, the thin hands and lithe beauty of the Vivien in *Merlin's Dream*. And it has always been so. A great artist invents a type, and Life tries to copy it, to reproduce it in a popular form, like an enterprising publisher. Neither Holbein nor Vandyck found in England

what they have given us. They brought their
types with them, and Life, with her keen imitative
faculty, set herself to supply the master with
models. The Greeks, with their quick artistic instinct, understood this, and set in the bride's chamber the statue of Hermes or of Apollo, that she
might bear children as lovely as the works of art
that she looked at in her rapture or her pain.
They knew that Life gains from Art not merely
spirituality, depth of thought and feeling, soul-
turmoil or soul-peace, but that she can form herself
on the very lines and colours of art and can reproduce the dignity of Pheidias as well as the grace of
Praxiteles. Hence came their objection to realism.
They disliked it on purely social grounds. They
felt that it inevitably makes people ugly, and they
were perfectly right. We try to improve the conditions of the race by means of good air, free sunlight, wholesome water, and hideous bare buildings
for the better housing of the lower orders. But
these things merely produce health; they do not
produce beauty. For this, Art is required, and the
true disciples of the great artist are not his studio-
imitators, but those who become like his works of
art, be they plastic as in Greek days, or pictorial as
in modern times; in a word, Life is Art's best,
Art's only pupil.

As it is with the visible arts, so it is with literature.  The most obvious and the vulgarest form in
which this is shown is in the case of the silly boys
who, after reading the adventures of Jack Sheppard
or Dick Turpin, pillage the stalls of unfortunate
apple-women, break into sweet-shops at night, and
alarm old gentlemen who are returning home from
the city by leaping out on them in suburban lanes,
with black masks and unloaded revolvers.  This
interesting phenomenon, which always occurs after
the appearance of a new edition of either of the
books I have alluded to, is usually attributed to the
influence of literature on the imagination.  But this
is a mistake.  The imagination is essentially creative
and always seeks for a new form.  The boy-burglar
is simply the inevitable result of life's imitative instinct.  He is Fact, occupied as Fact usually is
with trying to reproduce Fiction, and what we see
in him is repeated on an extended scale throughout
the whole of life.  Schopenhauer has analysed the
pessimism that characterises modern thought, but
Hamlet invented it.  The world has become sad
because a puppet was once melancholy.  The Nihi-
list, that strange martyr who has no faith, who goes
to the stake without enthusiasm, and dies for what
he does not believe in, is a purely literary product.
He was invented by Tourgénieff, and completed by

Dostoieffski.   Robespierre came out of the pages of
Rousseau as surely as the People's Palace rose out
débris of a novel.   Literature always anticipates
life.   It does not copy it, but moulds it to its purpose.   The nineteenth century, as we know it, is
largely an invention of Balzac.   Our Luciens de
Rubempré, our Rastignacs, and De Marsays made
their first appearance on the stage of the *Comédie
Humaine*.   We are merely carrying out, with foot-
notes and unnecessary additions, the whim or fancy
or creative vision of a great novelist.   I once asked
a lady, who knew Thackeray intimately, whether
he had had any model for Becky Sharp.   She told
me that Becky was an invention, but that the idea
of the character had been partly suggested by a
governess who lived in the neighbourhood of Ken-
sington Square, and was the companion of a very
selfish and rich old woman.   I inquired what became of the governess, and she replied that, oddly
enough, some years after the appearance of *Vanity
Fair*, she ran away with the nephew of the lady
with whom she was living, and for a short time
made a great splash in society, quite in Mrs. Rawdon Crawley's style, and entirely by Mrs. Rawdon
Crawley's methods.   Ultimately she came to grief,
disappeared to the Continent, and used to be occasionally seen at Monte Carlo and other gambling

places.   The noble gentleman from whom the same
great sentimentalist drew Colonel Newcome died, a
few months after *The Newcomes* had reached a
fourth edition, with the word " Adsum " on his lips.
Shortly after Mr. Stevenson published his curious
psychological story of transformation, a friend of
mine, called Mr. Hyde, was in the north of London,
and being anxious to get to a railway station, took
what he thought would be a short cut, lost his way,
and found himself in a network of mean, evil-look-
ing streets.   Feeling rather nervous he began to
walk extremely fast, when suddenly out of an arch-
way ran a child right between his legs.   It fell on
the pavement, he tripped over it, and trampled upon
it.   Being of course very much frightened and a
little hurt, it began to scream, and in a few seconds
the whole street was full of rough people who came
pouring out of the houses like ants.   They sur-
rounded him, and asked him his name.  He was just
about to give it when he suddenly remembered the
opening incident in Mr. Stevenson's story.  He was
so filled with horror at having realized in his own
person that terrible and well written scene, and at
having done accidentally, though in fact, what the
Mr. Hyde of fiction had done with deliberate intent,
that he ran away as hard as he could go.   He was,
however, very closely followed, and finally he took

refuge in a surgery, the door of which happened to
be open, where he explained to a young assistant,
who was serving there, exactly what had occurred.
The humanitarian crowd were induced to go away
on his giving them a small sum of money, and as
soon as the coast was quite clear he left.  As he
passed out, the name on the brass door-plate of the
surgery caught his eye.  It was "Jekyll."  At
least it should have been.

Here the imitation, as far as it went, was of
course accidental.  In the following case the imitation was self-conscious.  In the year 1879, just after
I had left Oxford, I met at a reception at the house
of one of the Foreign Ministers a woman of very
curious exotic beauty.  We became great friends,
and were constantly together.  And yet what interested most in her was not her beauty, but her
character, her entire vagueness of character.  She
seemed to have no personality at all, but simply the
possibility of many types.  Sometimes she would
give herself up entirely to art, turn her drawing-
room into a studio, and spend two or three days a
week at picture-galleries or museums.  Then she
would take to attending race-meetings, wear the
most horsey clothes, and talk about nothing but
betting.  She abandoned religion for mesmerism,
mesmerism for politics, and politics for the melodra-

matic excitements of philanthropy.   In fact, she
was a kind of Proteus, and as much a failure in all
her transformations as was that wondrous sea-god
when Odysseus laid hold of him.   One day a serial
began in one of the French magazines.   At that
time I used to read serial stories, and I well remember the shock of surprise I felt when I came to the
description of the heroine.   She was so like my
friend that I brought her the magazine, and she recognized herself in it immediately, and seemed fascinated by the resemblance.   I should tell you, by
the way, that the story was translated from some
dead Russian writer, so that the author had not
taken his type from my friend.   Well, to put the
matter briefly, some months afterwards I was in
Venice, and finding the magazine in the reading-
room of the hotel, I took it up casually to see what
had become of the heroine.   It was a most piteous
tale, as the girl had ended by running away with a
man absolutely inferior to her, not merely in social
station, but in character and intellect also.   I wrote
to my friend that evening about my views on John
Bellini, and the admirable ices at Florio's, and the
artistic value of gondolas, but added a postscript
to the effect that her double in the story had be-
haved in a very silly manner.   I don't know why I
added that, but I remember I had a sort of dread

over me that she might do the same thing. Before
my letter had reached her, she had run away with
a man who deserted her in six months.  I saw her
in 1884 in Paris, where she was living with her
mother, and I asked her whether the story had had
anything to do with her action.  She told me that
she had felt an absolutely irresistible impulse
to follow the heroine step by step in her strange
and fatal progress, and that it was with a feeling of
real terror that she had looked forward to the last
few chapters of the story.  When they appeared,
it seemed to her that she was compelled to reproduce them in life, and she did so.  It was a most
clear example of this imitative instinct of which I
was speaking, and an extremely tragic one.

However, I do not wish to dwell any further upon
individual instances.  Personal experience is a most
vicious and limited circle.  All that I desire to point
out is the general principle that Life imitates Art
far more than Art imitates Life, and I feel sure that
if you think seriously about it you will find that it
is true.  Life holds the mirror up to Art, and either
reproduces some strange type imagined by painter
or sculptor, or realizes in fact what has been dreamed
in fiction.  Scientifically speaking, the basis of life—
the energy of life, as Aristotle would call it—is
simply the desire for expression, and Art is always

presenting various forms through which this expression can be attained.    Life seizes on them and
uses them, even if they be to her own hurt.    Young
men have committed suicide because Rolla did so,
have died by their own hand because by his own
hand Werther died.    Think of what we owe to the
imitation of Christ, of what we owe to the imitation
of Cæsar.

*Cyril.* The theory is certainly a very curious one,
but to make it complete you must show that Nature,
no less than Life, is an imitation of Art.    Are you
prepared to prove that?

*Vivian.* My dear fellow, I am prepared to prove
anything.

*Cyril.* Nature follows the landscape painter then,
and takes her effects from him?

*Vivian.* Certainly.    Where, if not from the Impressionists, do we get those wonderful brown fogs
that come creeping down our streets, blurring the
gas-lamps and changing the houses into monstrous
shadows?    To whom, if not to them and their master,
do we owe the lovely silver mists that brood over our
river, and turn to faint forms of fading grace curved
bridge and swaying barge?    The extraordinary
change that has taken place in the climate of London
during the last ten years is entirely due to this
particular school of Art.    You smile.    Consider the

matter from a scientific or a metaphysical point of view, and you will find that I am right. For what is Nature? Nature is no great mother who has borne us. She is our creation. It is in our brain that she quickens to life. Things are because we see them, and what we see, and how we see it, depends on the Arts that have influenced us. To look at a thing is very different from seeing a thing. One does not see anything until one sees its beauty. Then, and then only, does it come into existence. At present, people see fogs, not because there are fogs, but because poets and painters have taught them the mysterious loveliness of such effects. There may have been fogs for centuries in London. I dare say there were. But no one saw them, and so we do not know anything about them. They did not exist till Art had invented them. Now, it must be admitted, fogs are carried to excess. They have become the mere mannerism of a clique, and the exaggerated realism of their method gives dull people bronchitis. Where the cultured catch an effect, the uncultured catch cold. And so, let us be humane, and invite Art to turn her wonderful eyes elsewhere. She has done so already, indeed. That white quivering sunlight that one sees now in France, with its strange blotches of mauve, and its restless violet shadows, is her latest fancy, and, on the whole,

Nature reproduces it quite admirably. Where she used to give us Corots and Daubignys, she gives us now exquisite Monets and entrancing Pisaros. Indeed there are moments, rare, it is true, but still to be observed from time to time, when Nature becomes absolutely modern. Of course she is not always to be relied upon. The fact is that she is in this unfortunate position. Art creates an incomparable and unique effect, and, having done so, passes on to other things. Nature, upon the other hand, forgetting that imitation can be made the sincerest form of insult, keeps on repeating this effect until we all become absolutely wearied of it. Nobody of any real culture, for instance, ever talks now-a-days about the beauty of a sunset. Sunsets are quite old-fashioned. They belong to the time when Turner was the last note in art. To admire them is a distinct sign of provincialism of temperament. Upon the other hand they go on. Yesterday evening Mrs. Arundel insisted on my coming to the window, and looking at the glorious sky, as she called it. Of course I had to look at it. She is one of those absurdly pretty Philistines, to whom one can deny nothing. And what was it? It was simply a very second-rate Turner, a Turner of a bad period, with all the painter's worst faults exaggerated and over-emphasized. Of course, I am quite ready to

admit that Life very often commits the same error.
She produces her false Renés and her sham Vautrins,
just as Nature gives us, on one day a doubtful Cuyp,
and on another a more than questionable Rousseau.
Still, Nature irritates one more when she does things
of that kind.    It seems so stupid, so obvious, so unnecessary.    A false Vautrin might be delightful.    A
doubtful Cuyp is unbearable.    However, I don't
want to be too hard on Nature.    I wish the Channel,
especially at Hastings, did not look quite so often
like a Henry Moore, grey pearl with yellow lights,
but then, when Art is more varied, Nature will, no
doubt, be more varied also.    That she imitates Art,
I don't think even her worst enemy would deny
now.    It is the one thing that keeps her in touch
with civilized man.    But have I proved my theory
to your satisfaction?

*Cyril.* You have proved it to my dissatisfaction,
which is better.    But even admitting this strange
imitative instinct in Life and Nature, surely you
would acknowledge that Art expresses the temper
of its age, the spirit of its time, the moral and social
conditions that surround it, and under whose influence it is produced.

*Vivian.* Certainly not!    Art never expresses anything but itself.    This is the principle of my new
æsthetics; and it is this, more than that vital con-

nection between form and substance, on which Mr.
Pater dwells, that makes music the type of all the
arts.  Of course, nations and individuals, with that
healthy, natural vanity which is the secret of existence, are always under the impression that it is of
them that the Muses are talking, always trying to
find in the calm dignity of imaginative art some
mirror of their own turbid passions, always forgetting that the singer of Life is not Apollo, but
Marsyas.  Remote from reality, and with her eyes
turned away from the shadows of the cave, Art reveals her own perfection, and the wondering crowd
that watches the opening of the marvellous, many-
petalled rose fancies that it is its own history that is
being told to it, its own spirit that is finding expression in a new form.  But it is not so.  The
highest art rejects the burden of the human spirit,
and gains more from a new medium or a fresh
material than she does from any enthusiasm for
art, or from any lofty passion, or from any great
awakening of the human consciousness.  She develops purely on her own lines.  She is not sym-
bolic of any age.  It is the ages that are her symbols.

Even those who hold that Art is representative of
time and place and people, cannot help admitting
that the more imitative an art is, the less it repre-

sents to us the spirit of its age.   The evil faces of
the Roman emperors look out at us from the foul
porphyry and spotted jasper in which the realistic
artists of the day delighted to work, and we fancy
that in those cruel lips and heavy sensual jaws we
can find the secret of the ruin of the Empire.   But
it was not so.   The vices of Tiberius could not destroy that supreme civilization, any more than the
virtues of the Antonines could save it.   It fell for
other, for less interesting reasons.   The sibyls and
prophets of the Sistine may indeed serve to interpret for some that new birth of the emancipated
spirit that we call the Renaissance; but what do the
drunken boors and brawling peasants of Dutch art
tell us about the great soul of Holland?   The more
abstract, the more ideal an art is, the more it reveals
to us the temper of its age.   If we wish to understand a nation by means of its art, let us look at its
architecture or its music.

*Cyril.* I quite agree with you there.   The spirit
of an age may be best expressed in the abstract
ideal arts, for the spirit itself is abstract and ideal.
Upon the other hand, for the visible aspect of an
age, for its look, as the phrase goes, we must of
course go to the arts of imitation.

*Vivian.* I don't think so.   After all, what the
imitative arts really give us are merely the various

styles of particular artists, or of certain schools of
artists. Surely you don't imagine that the people of
the Middle Ages bore any resemblance at all to the
figures on mediæval stained glass or in mediæval
stone and wood carving, or on mediæval metal-
work, or tapestries, or illuminated MSS. They were
probably very ordinary-looking people, with nothing grotesque, or remarkable, or fantastic in their
appearance. The Middle Ages, as we know them
in art, are simply a definite form of style, and there
is no reason at all why an artist with this style
should not be produced in the nineteenth century.
No great artist ever sees things as they really are.
If he did, he would cease to be an artist. Take
an example from our own day. I know that
you are fond of Japanese things. Now, do you
really imagine that the Japanese people, as they are
presented to us in art, have any existence? If you
do, you have never understood Japanese art at all.
The Japanese people are the deliberate self-conscious creation of certain individual artists. If you
set a picture by Hokusai, or Hokkei, or any of the
great native painters, beside a real Japanese gentleman or lady, you will see that there is not the
slightest resemblance between them. The actual
people who live in Japan are not unlike the general
run of English people; that is to say, they are ex-

tremely commonplace, and have nothing curious or
extraordinary about them.   In fact the whole of
Japan is a pure invention.   There is no such country, there are no such people.   One of our most
charming painters went recently to the Land of the
Chrysanthemum in the foolish hope of seeing the
Japanese.   All he saw, all he had the chance of
painting, were a few lanterns and some fans.   He
was quite unable to discover the inhabitants, as his
delightful exhibition at Messrs. Dowdeswell's Gallery showed only too well.   He did not know that
the Japanese people are, as I have said, simply a
mode of style, an exquisite fancy of art.   And so,
if you desire to see a Japanese effect, you will not
behave like a tourist and go to Tokio.   On the con-
trary, you will stay at home, and steep yourself in
the work of certain Japanese artists, and then, when
you have absorbed the spirit of their style, and
caught their imaginative manner of vision, you will
go some afternoon and sit in the Park or stroll down
Piccadilly, and if you cannot see an absolutely Japanese effect there, you will not see it anywhere.
Or, to return again to the past, take as another instance the ancient Greeks.   Do you think that
Greek art ever tells us what the Greek people
were like?   Do you believe that the Athenian
women were like the stately dignified figures of the

Parthenon frieze, or like those marvellous goddesses who sat in the triangular pediments of the same building? If you judge from the art, they certainly were so. But read an authority, like Aristophanes for instance. You will find that the Athenian ladies laced tightly, wore high-heeled shoes, died their hair yellow, painted and rouged their faces, and were exactly like any silly fashionable or fallen creature of our own day. The fact is that we look back on the ages entirely through the medium of Art, and Art, very fortunately, has never once told us the truth.

*Cyril.* But modern portraits by English painters, what of them? Surely they are like the people they pretend to represent?

*Vivian.* Quite so. They are so like them that a hundred years from now no one will believe in them. The only portraits in which one believes are portraits where there is very little of the sitter and a very great deal of the artist. Holbein's drawings of the men and women of his time impress us with a sense of their absolute reality. But this is simply because Holbein compelled life to accept his conditions, to restrain itself within his limitations, to reproduce his type, and to appear as he wished it to appear. It is style that makes us believe in a thing—nothing but style. Most of our modern portrait painters are

doomed to absolute oblivion. They never paint
what they see. They paint what the public sees,
and the public never sees anything.

*Cyril.* Well, after that I think I should like to hear
the end of your article.

*Vivian.* With pleasure. Whether it will do any
good I really cannot say. Ours is certainly the dull-
est and most prosaic century possible. Why, even
Sleep has played us false, and has closed up the gates
of ivory, and opened the gates of horn. The dreams
of the great middle classes of this country, as recorded in Mr. Myers's two bulky volumes on the subject and in the Transactions of the Psychical Society,
are the most depressing things that I have ever read.
There is not even a fine nightmare among them.
They are commonplace, sordid, and tedious. As for
the Church I cannot conceive anything better for the
culture of a country than the presence in it of a
body of men whose duty it is to believe in the super-
natural, to perform daily miracles, and to keep alive
that mythopœic faculty which is so essential for the
imagination. But in the English Church a man succeeds, not through his capacity for belief but through
his capacity for disbelief. Ours is the only Church
where the sceptic stands at the altar, and where St.
Thomas is regarded as the ideal apostle. Many a
worthy clergyman, who passes his life in admirable

works of kindly charity, lives and dies unnoticed and unknown; but it is sufficient for some shallow uneducated passman out of either University to get up in his pulpit and express his doubts about Noah's ark, or Balaam's ass, or Jonah and the whale, for half of London to flock to hear him, and to sit open-mouthed in rapt admiration at his superb intellect. The growth of common sense in the English Church is a thing very much to be regretted. It is really a degrading concession to a low form of realism. It is silly, too. It springs from an entire ignorance of psychology. Man can believe the impossible, but man can never believe the improbable. However, I must read the end of my article : —

" What we have to do, what at any rate it is our duty to do, is to revive this old art of Lying. Much of course may be done, in the way of educating the public, by amateurs in the domestic circle, at literary lunches, and at afternoon teas. But this is merely the light and graceful side of lying, such as was probably heard at Cretan dinner parties. There are many other forms. Lying for the sake of gaining some immediate personal advantage, for instance— lying with a moral purpose, as it is usually called— though of late it has been rather looked down upon, was extremely popular with the antique world. Athena laughs when Odysseus tells her ' his words of sly devising,' as Mr. William Morris phrases it, and the glory of mendacity illumines the pale brow of the stainless hero of Euripidean tragedy, and sets among the noble women of the past the young bride of one of Horace's most exquisite odes. Later on, what at first had been merely a natural instinct was elevated into a self-conscious science. Elaborate rules were laid down for the guidance of mankind, and an important school of literature grew up round the subject. Indeed, when one remembers the excellent philosophical treatise of Sanchez on the whole question one cannot help regretting that no one has ever thought of publishing a cheap and condensed edition of the works of that great casuist. A short primer, ' When to Lie and How,' if brought out in an attractive and not too expensive a form, would no doubt command a large sale, and would prove of real practical service to many earnest and deep-thinking people. Lying for the sake of the improvement of the young, which is the basis of home education, still lingers amongst us, and its advantages are so admirably set forth in the early books of Plato's *Republic* that it is unnecessary to dwell upon them here. It is a mode of lying for which all good mothers have peculiar capabilities, but it is capable of still further development, and has been sadly overlooked by the School Board. Lying for the sake of a monthly sal-

ary is of course well known in Fleet Street, and the
profession of a political leader-writer is not without
its advantages.    But it is said to be a somewhat dull
occupation, and it certainly does not lead to much
beyond a kind of ostentatious obscurity.   The only
form of lying that is absolutely beyond reproach is
Lying for its own sake, and the highest development
of this is, as we have already pointed out, Lying in
Art.   Just as those who do not love Plato more than
Truth cannot pass beyond the threshold of the
Academe, so those who do not love Beauty more
than Truth never know the inmost shrine of Art. The
solid stolid British intellect lies in the desert sands
like the Sphinx in Flaubert's marvellous tale, and
fantasy *La Chimère*, dances round it, and calls to it
with her false, flute-toned voice.   It may not hear
her now, but surely some day, when we are all bored
to death with the commonplace character of modern
fiction, it will hearken to her and try to borrow her
wings.

" And when that day dawns, or sunset reddens how
joyous we shall all be!   Facts will be regarded as
discreditable, Truth will be found mourning over her
fetters, and Romance, with her temper of wonder,
will  return  to  the  land.   The  very  aspect  of  the
world will change to our startled eyes.   Out of the
sea will rise Behemoth and Leviathan, and sail round

the high-pooped galleys, as they do on the delightful maps of those ages when books on geography
were actually readable.    Dragons will wander about
the waste places, and the phœnix will soar from her
nest of fire into the air.    We shall lay our hands
upon the basilisk, and see the jewel in the toad's head.
Champing his gilded oats, the Hippogriff will stand
in our stalls, and over our heads will float the Blue
Bird singing of beautiful and impossible things, of
things that are lovely and that never happened, of
things that are not and that should be.    But before
this comes to pass we must cultivate the lost art of
Lying."

*Cyril.*  Then we must certainly cultivate it at once.
But in order to avoid making any error I want you to
tell me briefly the doctrines of the new æsthetics.

*Vivian.*  Briefly, then, they are these.    Art never
expresses anything but itself.    It has an independent life, just as Thought has, and develops purely on
its own lines.    It is not necessarily realistic in an
age of realism, nor spiritual in an age of faith.    So
far from being the creation of its time, it is usually in
direct opposition to it, and the only history that it
preserves for us is the history of its own progress.
Sometimes it returns upon its footsteps, and revives
some antique form, as happened in the archaistic
movement of late Greek Art, and in the pre-Ra-

phaelite movement of our own day. At other times it entirely anticipates its age, and produces in one century work that it takes another century to understand, to appreciate, and to enjoy. In no case does it reproduce its age. To pass from the art of a time to the time itself is the great mistake that all historians commit.

The second doctrine is this. All bad art comes from returning to Life and Nature, and elevating them into ideals. Life and Nature may sometimes be used as part of Art's rough material, but before they are of any real service to art they must be translated into artistic conventions. The moment Art surrenders its imaginative medium it surrenders everything. As a method Realism is a complete failure, and the two things that every artist should avoid are modernity of form and modernity of subject-matter. To us, who live in the nineteenth century, any century is a suitable subject for art except our own. The only beautiful things are the things that do not concern us. It is, to have the pleasure of quoting myself, exactly because Hecuba is nothing to us that her sorrows are so suitable a motive for a tragedy. Besides, it is only the modern that ever becomes old-fashioned. M. Zola sits down to give us a picture of the Second Empire. Who cares for the Second Empire now? It is out of date. Life goes faster than Realism, but Romanticism is always in front of Life.

The third doctrine is that Life imitates Art far more than Art imitates Life. This results not merely from Life's imitative instinct, but from the fact that the self-conscious aim of Life is to find expression, and that Art offers it certain beautiful forms through which it may realize that energy. It is a theory that has never been put forward before, but it is extremely fruitful, and throws an entirely new light upon the history of Art.

It follows, as a corollary from this, that external Nature also imitates Art. The only effects that she can show us are effects that we have already seen through poetry, or in paintings. This is the secret of Nature's charm, as well as the explanation of Nature's weakness.

The final revelation is that Lying, the telling of beautiful untrue things, is the proper aim of Art. But of this I think I have spoken at sufficient length. And now let us go out on the terrace, where "droops the milk-white peacock like a ghost," while the evening star " washes the dusk with silver." At twilight nature becomes a wonderfully suggestive effect, and is not without loveliness, though perhaps its chief use is to illustrate quotations from the poets. Come! We have talked long enough.

# PEN PENCIL AND POISON

## A STUDY IN GREEN

# PEN PENCIL AND POISON

It has constantly been made a subject of reproach against artists and men of letters that they are lacking in wholeness and completeness of nature.  As a rule this must necessarily be so.  That very concentration of vision and intensity of purpose which is the characteristic of the artistic temperament is in itself a mode of limitation.  To those who are preoccupied with the beauty of form nothing else seems of much importance.  Yet there are many exceptions to this rule.  Rubens served as ambassador, and Goethe as state councillor, and Milton as Latin secretary to Cromwell.  Sophocles held civic office in his own city; the humourists, essayists, and novelists of modern America seem to desire nothing better than to become the diplomatic representatives of their country; and Charles Lamb's friend, Thomas Griffiths Wainewright, the subject of this brief memoir, though of an extremely artistic temperament, fol-

lowed many masters other than art, being not
merely a poet and a painter and an art-critic, an
antiquarian, and a writer of prose, an amateur of
beautiful things, and a dilettante of things delightful, but also a forger of no mean or ordinary capabilities, and as a subtle and secret poisoner almost
without rival in this or any age.

This remarkable man, so powerful with "pen,
pencil, and poison," as a great poet of our own day
has finely said of him, was born at Chiswick, in 1794.
His father was the son of a distinguished solicitor of
Gray's Inn and Hatton Garden. His mother was
the daughter of the celebrated Dr. Griffiths, the
editor and founder of the *Monthly Review*, the
partner in another literary speculation of Thomas
Davies, that famous bookseller of whom Johnson said
that he was not a bookseller, but "a gentleman who
dealt in books," the friend of Goldsmith and Wedg-
wood, and one of the most well-known men of his
day. Mrs. Wainewright died, in giving him birth,
at the early age of twenty-one, and an obituary
notice in the *Gentleman's Magazine* tells us of her
"amiable disposition and numerous accomplish-
ments," and adds somewhat quaintly that "she is
supposed to have understood the writings of Mr.
Locke as well as perhaps any person of either sex
now living." His father did not long survive his

young wife, and the little child seems to have been
brought up by his grandfather, and, on the death
of the latter in 1803, by his uncle George Edward
Griffiths, whom he subsequently poisoned.  His
boyhood was passed at Linden House, Turnham
Green, one of those many fine Georgian mansions
that have unfortunately disappeared before the in-
roads of the suburban builder, and to its lovely
gardens and well-timbered park he owed that simple
and impassioned love of nature which never left him
all through his life, and which made him so peculiarly
susceptible to the spiritual influences of Wordsworth's poetry.  He went to school at Charles
Burney's academy at Hammersmith.  Mr. Burney
was the son of the historian of music, and the near
kinsman of the artistic lad who was destined to turn
out his most remarkable pupil.  He seems to have
been a man of a good deal of culture, and in after
years Mr. Wainewright often spoke of him with much
affection as a philosopher, an archæologist, and an
admirable teacher who, while he valued the intellectual side of education, did not forget the importance of early moral training.  It was under Mr.
Burney that he first developed his talent as an artist,
and Mr. Hazlitt tells us that a drawing book which
he used at school is still extant, and displays great
talent and natural feeling.  Indeed, painting was

the first art that fascinated him. It was not till much later that he sought to find expression by pen or poison.

Before this, however, he seems to have been carried away by boyish dreams of the romance and chivalry of a soldier's life, and to have become a young guardsman. But the reckless dissipated life of his companions failed to satisfy the refined artistic temperament of one who was made for other things. In a short time he wearied of the service. " Art," he tells us, in words that still move many by their ardent sincerity and strange fervour, "Art touched her renegade; by her pure and high influences the noisome mists were purged; my feelings, parched, hot, and tarnished, were renovated with cool, fresh bloom, simple, beautiful to the simple-hearted." But Art was not the only cause of the change. " The writings of Wordsworth," he goes on to say, " did much towards calming the confusing whirl necessarily incident to sudden mutations. I wept over them tears of happiness and gratitude." He accordingly left the army, with its rough barrack-life and coarse mess-room tittle-tattle, and returned to Linden House, full of this new-born enthusiasm for culture. A severe illness, in which, to use his own words, he was " broken like a vessel of clay," prostrated him for a time. His

delicately strung organization, however indifferent
it might have been to inflicting pain on others, was
itself most keenly sensitive to pain.  He shrank
from suffering as a thing that mars and maims
human life, and seems to have wandered through
that terrible valley of melancholia from which so
many great, perhaps greater, spirits have never
emerged.  But he was young—only twenty-five
years of age—and he soon passed out of the " dead
black waters," as he called them, into the larger
air of humanistic culture.  As he was recovering
from the illness that had led him almost to the
gates of death, he conceived the idea of taking up
literature as an art.  " I said with John Woodvill,"
he cries, " it were a life of gods to dwell in such an
element," to see, and hear, and write brave
things: —

> " These high and gusty relishes of life
>   Have no allayings of mortality."

It is impossible not to feel that in this passage
we have the utterance of a man who had a true
passion for letters.  " To see, and hear, and write
brave things," this was his aim.

Scott, the editor of the *London Magazine*, struck
by the young man's genius, or under the influence
of the strange fascination that he exercised on every

one who knew him, invited him to write a series of articles on artistic subjects, and under a series of fanciful pseudonyms he began to contribute to the literature of his day. *Janus Weathercock, Egomet Bonmot,* and *Van Vinkvooms,* were some of the grotesque masks under which he chose to hide his seriousness, or to reveal his levity. A mask tells us more than a face. These disguises intensified his personality. In an incredibly short time he seems to have made his mark. Charles Lamb speaks of "kind, light-hearted Wainewright," whose prose is "capital." We hear of him entertaining Macready, John Forster, Maginn, Talfourd, Sir Wentworth Dilke, the poet John Clare, and others, at a *petit-dîner.* Like Disraeli, he determined to startle the town as a dandy, and his beautiful rings, his antique cameo breast-pin, and his pale lemon-coloured kid gloves, were well known, and indeed were regarded by Hazlitt as being the signs of a new manner in literature: while his rich curly hair, fine eyes, and exquisite white hands gave him the dangerous and delightful distinction of being different from others. There was something in him of Balzac's Lucien de Rubempré. At times he reminds us of Julien Sorel. De Quincy saw him once. It was at a dinner at Charles Lamb's. "Amongst the company, all literary

men, sat a murderer," he tells us, and he goes on
to describe how on that day he had been ill, and
had hated the face of man and woman, and yet
found himself looking with intellectual interest
across the table at the young writer beneath whose
affectations of manner there seemed to him to lie
so much unaffected sensibility, and speculates on
"what sudden growth of another interest," would
have changed his mood, had he known of what
terrible sin the guest to whom Lamb paid so much
attention was even then guilty.

His life-work falls naturally under the three heads
suggested by Mr. Swinburne, and it may be partly
admitted that, if we set aside his achievements in
the sphere of poison, what he has actually left to us
hardly justifies his reputation.

But then it is only the Philistine who seeks to
estimate a personality by the vulgar test of production.   This young dandy sought to be somebody,
rather than to do something.   He recognized that
Life itself is an art, and has its modes of style no
less than the arts that seek to express it.   Nor is
his work without interest.   We hear of William
Blake stopping in the Royal Academy before one
of his pictures and pronouncing it to be "very
fine."   His essays are prefiguring of much that has
since been realized.   He seems to have anticipated

some of those accidents of modern culture that are
regarded by many as true essentials. He writes
about La Gioconda, and early French poets and the
Italian Renaissance. He loves Greek gems, and
Persian carpets, and Elizabethan translations of *Cupid
and Psyche*, and the *Hypnerotomachia*, and book-
bindings, and early editions, and wide-margined
proofs. He is keenly sensitive to the value of
beautiful surroundings, and never wearies of de-
scribing to us the rooms in which he lived, or
would have liked to live. He had that curious love
of green, which in individuals is always the sign of
a subtle artistic temperament, and in nations is said
to denote a laxity, if not a decadence of morals.
Like Baudelaire, he was extremely fond of cats, and
with Gautier, he was fascinated by that "sweet
marble monster" of both sexes that we can still see
at Florence and in the Louvre.

There is of course much in his descriptions, and
his suggestions for decoration, that shows that he
did not entirely free himself from the false taste
of his time. But it is clear that he was one of the
first to recognize what is, indeed, the very keynote
of æsthetic eclecticism, I mean the true harmony
of all really beautiful things irrespective of age or
place, of school or manner. He saw that in deco-
rating a room, which is to be, not a room for show,

but a room to live in, we should never aim at any
archæological reconstruction of the past, nor burden
ourselves with any fanciful necessity for historical
accuracy. In this artistic perception he was perfectly right. All beautiful things belong to the
same age.

And so, in his own library, as he describes it, we
find the delicate fictile vase of the Greek, with its
exquisitely painted figures and the faint ΚΑΛΟΣ
finely traced upon its side, and behind it hangs an
engraving of the " Delphic Sibyl " of Michael
Angelo, or of the " Pastoral " of Giorgione. Here
is a bit of Florentine majolica, and here a rude
lamp from some old Roman tomb. On the table
lies a book of Hours " cased in a cover of solid silver
gilt, wrought with quaint devices and studded with
small brilliants and rubies," and close by it " squats
a little ugly monster, a Lar, perhaps, dug up in the
sunny fields of corn-bearing Sicily." Some dark
antique bronzes contrast " with the pale gleam of
two noble *Christi Crucifixi*, one carved in ivory,
the other moulded in wax." He has his trays of
Tassie's gems, his tiny Louis-Quatorze *bonbonnière*
with a miniature by Petitot, his highly prized
" brown-biscuit teapots, filagree-worked," his citron
morocco letter-case, and his " pomona-green "
chair.

One can fancy him lying there in the midst of his
books and casts and engravings, a true virtuoso, a
subtle connoisseur, turning over his fine collection
of Marc Antonios, and his Turner's "Liber Stu-
diorum," of which he was a warm admirer, or ex-
amining with a magnifier some of his antique gems
and cameos, " the head of Alexander on an onyx of
two strata," or that superb *altissimo relievo* on cor-
nelian, Jupiter Ægiochus." He was always a great
amateur of engravings, and gives some very useful
suggestions as to the best means of forming a collection. Indeed, while fully appreciating modern
art, he never lost sight of the importance of reproductions of the great masterpieces of the past, and
all that he says about the value of plaster casts is
quite admirable.

As an art-critic he concerned himself primarily
with the complex impressions produced by a work
of art, and certainly the first step in æsthetic criticism is to realize one's own impressions. He cared
nothing for abstract discussions on the nature of the
Beautiful, and the historical method, which has since
yielded such rich fruit, did not belong to his day,
but he never lost sight of the great truth that Art's
first appeal is neither to the intellect nor to the emotions, but purely to the artistic temperament, and he
more than once points out that this temperament,

this "taste," as he calls it, being unconsciously guided
and made perfect by frequent contact with the best
work, becomes in the end a form of right judgment.
Of course there are fashions in art just as there are
fashions in dress, and perhaps none of us can ever
quite free ourselves from the influence of custom
and the influence of novelty.  He certainly could
not, and he frankly acknowledges how difficult it is
to form any fair estimate of contemporary work.
But, on the whole, his taste was good and sound.
He admired Turner and Constable at a time when
they were not so much thought of as they are now,
and saw that for the highest landscape art we require more than " mere industry and accurate tran-
scription."   Of Crome's " Heath Scene near Nor-
wich " he remarks that it shows " how much a
subtle observation of the elements, in their wild
moods, does for a most uninteresting flat," and of
the popular type of landscape of his day he says
that is " simply an enumeration of hill and dale,
stumps of trees, shrubs, water, meadows, cottages,
and houses ; little more than topography, a kind of
pictorial map-work ; in which rainbows, showers,
mists, haloes, large beams shooting through rifted
clouds, storms, starlight, all the most valued materials of the real painter, are not."  He had a thor
ough  dislike of what is obvious or commonplace in

art, and while he was charmed to entertain Wilkie
at dinner, he cared as little for Sir David's pictures
as he did for Mr. Crabbe's poems.  With the imitative and realistic tendencies of his day he had no
sympathy, and he tells us frankly that his great
admiration for Fuseli was largely due to the fact
that the little Swiss did not consider it necessary
that an artist should only paint what he sees.  The
qualities that he sought for in a picture were composition, beauty and dignity of line, richness of
colour, and imaginative power.  Upon the other
hand, he was not a doctrinaire.  " I hold that no
work of art can be tried otherwise than by laws de-
duced from itself: whether or not it be consistent
with itself is the question."  This is one of his excellent aphorisms.  And in criticising painters so
different as Landseer and Martin, Stothard and
Etty, he shows that, to use a phrase now classical,
he is trying " to see the object as in itself it
really is."

However, as I pointed out before, he never feels
quite at his ease in his criticisms of contemporary
work.  " The present," he says, " is about as agree-
able a confusion to me as Ariosto on the first peru-
sal. . . . Modern things dazzle me.  I must look
at them through Time's telescope.  Elia complains
that to him the merit of a MS. poem is uncertain;

'print,' as he excellently says, 'settles it.' Fifty
years' toning does the same thing to a picture."
He is happier when he is writing about Watteau
and Lancret, about Rubens and Giorgione, about
Rembrandt, Correggio and Michael Angelo; hap-
piest of all when he is writing about Greek things.
What is Gothic touched him very little, but classical
art and the art of the Renaissance were always dear
to him.  He saw what our English school could
gain from a study of Greek models, and never
wearies of pointing out to the young student the
artistic possibilities that lie dormant in Hellenic
marbles and Hellenic methods of work.  In his
judgments on the great Italian Masters, says De
Quincey, "There seemed a tone of sincerity and
of native sensibility, as in one who spoke for himself, and was not merely a copier from books."
The highest praise that we can give to him is that
he tried to revive style as a conscious tradition.  But
he saw that no amount of art-lectures or art con-
gresses, or "plans for advancing the fine arts," will
ever produce this result.  The people, he says very
wisely, and in the true spirit of Toynbee Hall,
must always have "the best models constantly
before their eyes."
    As is to be expected from one who was a
painter, he is often extremely technical in his art

criticisms.  Of Tintoret's "St. George delivering
the Egyptian Princess from the Dragon " he remarks: —

> " The robe of Sabra, warmly glazed with Prussian blue, is
> relieved from the pale greenish background by a vermilion
> scarf; and the full hues of both are beautifully echoed, as it
> were, in a lower key by the purple-lake coloured stuffs and
> bluish iron armour of the saint, besides an ample balance to
> the vivid azure drapery on the foreground in the indigo
> shades of the wild wood surrounding the castle."

And elsewhere he talks learnedly of " a delicate
Schiavone, various as a tulip-bed, with rich broken
tints," of " a glowing portrait, remarkable for *mor-
bidezza*, by the scarce Moroni," and of another picture being " pulpy in the carnations."

But, as a rule, he deals with his impressions of
the work as an artistic whole, and tries to translate
those impressions into words, to give, as it were,
the literary equivalent for the imaginative and men-
tal effect.   He was one of the first to develop what
has been called the art-literature of the nineteenth
century, that form of literature which has found in
Mr. Ruskin and Mr. Browning its two most perfect
exponents.   His description of Lancret's *Repas
Italien*, in which " a dark-haired girl, 'amorous of
mischief,' lies on the daisy-powdered grass," is in
some respects very charming.   Here is his account

of "The Crucifixion," by Rembrandt.   It is extremely characteristic of his style:—

"Darkness—sooty, portentous darkness—shrouds the
whole scene: only above the accursed wood, as if through a
horrid rift in the murky ceiling, a rainy deluge—' sleety-
flaw, discoloured water'—streams down amain, spreading a
grisly spectral light, even more horrible than that palpable
night.   Already the Earth pants thick and fast! the dark-
ened Cross trembles! the winds are dropt—the air is stag-
nant—a muttering rumble growls underneath their feet, and
some of that miserable crowd begin to fly down the hill.   The
horses snuff the coming terror, and become unmanageable
through fear.   The moment rapidly approaches when, nearly
torn asunder by His own weight, fainting with loss of blood,
which now runs in narrower rivulets from His slit veins, His
temples and breast drowned in sweat, and His black tongue
parched with the fiery death-fever, Jesus cries, ' I thirst.'
The deadly vinegar is elevated to Him.

"His head sinks, and the sacred corpse 'swings sense-
less of the cross.'   A sheet of vermilion flame shoots sheer
through the air and vanishes; the rocks of Carmel and
Lebanon cleave asunder; the sea rolls on high from the
sands its black weltering waves.   Earth yawns, and the
graves give up their dwellers.   The dead and the living are
mingled together in unnatural conjunction and hurry through
the holy city.   New prodigies await them there.   The veil
of the temple—the unpierceable veil—is rent asunder from
top to bottom, and that dreaded recess containing the
Hebrew mysteries—the fatal ark with the tables and seven-
branched candelabrum—is disclosed by the light of unearthly
flames to the God-deserted multitude.

" Rembrandt never *painted* this sketch, and he was quite
right.   It would have lost nearly all its charms in losing that

perplexing veil of indistinctness which affords such ample range wherein the doubting imagination may speculate. At present it is like a thing in another world. A dark gulf is betwixt us. It is not tangible by the body. We can only approach it in the spirit."

In this passage, written, the author tells us, "in awe and reverence," there is much that is terrible, and very much that is quite horrible, but it is not without a certain crude form of power, or, at any rate, a certain crude violence of words, a quality which this age should highly appreciate, as it is its chief defect. It is pleasanter, however, to pass to this description of Giulio Romano's " Cephalus and Procris ":—

" We should read Moschus's lament for Bion, the sweet shepherd, before looking at this picture, or study the picture as a preparation for the lament. We have nearly the same images in both. For either victim the high groves and forest dells murmur; the flowers exhale sad perfume from their buds; the nightingale mourns on the craggy lands, and the swallow in the long-winding vales; ' the satyrs, too, and fauns dark-veiled groan,' and the fountain nymphs within the wood melt into tearful waters. The sheep and goats leave their pasture, and oreads, ' who love to scale the most inaccessible tops of all uprightest rocks,' hurry down from the song of their wind-courting pines; while the dryads bend from the branches of the meeting trees, and the rivers moan for white Procris, ' with many-sobbing streams,'

" Filling the far-seen ocean with a voice."

The golden bees are silent on the thymy Hymettus; and the

knelling horn of Aurora's love no more shall scatter away
the cold twilight on the top of Hymettus.   The foreground
of our subject is a grassy sunburnt bank, broken into swells
and hollows like waves (a sort of land-breakers), rendered
more uneven by many foot-tripping roots and stumps of trees
stocked untimely by the axe, which are again throwing out
light green shoots.   This bank rises rather suddenly on the
right to a clustering grove, penetrable to no star, at the entrance of which sits the stunned Thessalian king, holding between his knees that ivory-bright body which was, but an
instant agone, parting the rough boughs with her smooth
forehead, and treading alike on thorns and flowers with
jealousy-stung foot—now helpless, heavy, void of all motion, save when the breeze lifts her thick hair in mockery.

"From between the closely-neighboured boles astonished
nymphs press forward with loud cries—

"And deerskin-vested satyrs, crowned with ivy twists,
          advance ;
   And put strange pity in their horned countenance."

"Laelaps lies beneath, and shows by his panting the rapid
pace of death.   On the other side of the group, Virtuous
Love with 'vans dejected' holds forth the arrow to an approaching troop of sylvan people, fauns, rams, goats, satyrs,
and satyr-mothers, pressing their children tighter with their
fearful hands, who hurry along from the left in a sunken
path between the foreground and a rocky wall, on whose
lowest ridge a brook-guardian pours from her urn her grief-
telling waters. Above and more remote than the Ephidryad,
another female, rending her locks, appears among the vine-
festooned pillars of an unshorn grove.   The centre of the
picture is filled by shady meadows, sinking down to a river-
mouth ; beyond is ' the vast strength of the ocean stream,'
from whose floor the extinguisher of stars, rosy Aurora, drives

furiously up her brine-washed steeds to behold the death-pangs of her rival."

Were this description carefully rewritten, it would be quite admirable. The conception of making a prose-poem out of paint is excellent. Much of the best modern literature springs from the same aim. In a very ugly and sensible age, the arts borrow, not from life, but from each other.

His sympathies, too, were wonderfully varied. In everything connected with the stage, for instance, he was always extremely interested, and strongly up-held the necessity for archæological accuracy in costume and scene-painting. "In art," he says in one of his essays, "whatever is worth doing at all is worth doing well; " and he points out that once we allow the intrusion of anachronisms, it becomes difficult to say where the line is to be drawn. In literature, again, like Lord Beaconsfield on a famous occasion, he was "on the side of the angels." He was one of the first to admire Keats and Shelley— "the tremulously-sensitive and poetical Shelley," as he calls him. His admiration for Wordsworth was sincere and profound. He thoroughly appre-ciated William Blake. One of the best copies of the "Songs of Innocence and Experience" that is now in existence was wrought specially for him. He loved Alain Chartier, and Ronsard, and the

Elizabethan dramatists, and Chaucer and Chapman, and Petrarch. And to him all the arts were one. "Our critics," he remarks with much wisdom, "seem hardly aware of the identity of the primal seeds of poetry and painting, nor that any true advancement in the serious study of one art cogenerates a pro- portionate perfection in the other;" and he says elsewhere that if a man who does not admire Michael Angelo talks of his love for Milton, he is deceiving either himself or his listeners. To his fellow-contrib- utors in the *London Magazine* he was always most generous, and praises Barry Cornwall, Allan Cun- ningham, Hazlitt, Elton and Leigh Hunt without anything of the malice of a friend. Some of his sketches of Charles Lamb are admirable in their way, and, with the art of the true comedian, borrow their style from their subject : —

"What can I say of thee more than all know? that thou hadst the gaiety of a boy with the knowledge of a man: as gentle a heart as ever sent tears to the eyes.

"How wittily would he mistake your meaning, and put in a conceit most seasonably out of season. His talk without affectation was compressed, like his beloved Elizabethans, even unto obscurity. Like grains of fine gold, his sentences would beat out into whole sheets. He had small mercy on spurious fame, and a caustic observation on the *fashion for men of genius* was a standing dish. Sir Thomas Browne was a 'bosom cronie' of his; so was Burton, and old Fuller. In his amorous vein he dallied with that peerless Duchess of many-

folio odour; and with the heyday comedies of Beaumont and
Fletcher he induced light dreams.   He would deliver critical
touches on these, like one inspired, but it was good to let him
choose his own game; if another began even on the acknow-
ledged pets he was liable to interrupt, or rather append, in
a mode difficult to define whether as misapprehensive or
mischievous.   One night at C———'s, the above dramatic
partners were the temporary subject of chat.   Mr. X. com-
mended the passion and haughty style of a tragedy (I don't
know which of them), but was instantly taken up by Elia, who
told him ' *That* was nothing; the lyrics were the high things—
the lyrics ! ' "

One side of his literary career deserves especial
notice.   Modern journalism may be said to owe
almost as much to him as to any man of the early
part of this century.   He was the pioneer of Asiatic
prose, and delighted in pictorial epithets and pom-
pous exaggerations.   To have a style so gorgeous
that it conceals the subject is one of the highest
achievements of an important and much admired
school of Fleet Street leader-writers, and this school
*Janus Weathercock* may be said to have invented.
He also saw that it was quite easy by continued
reiteration to make the public interested in his own
personality, and in his purely journalistic articles
this extraordinary young man tells the world what
he had for dinner, where he gets his clothes, what
wines he likes, and in what state of health he is,
just as if he were writing weekly notes for some

popular newspaper of our own time. This being
the least valuable side of his work, is the one that
has had the most obvious influence. A publicist,
now-a-days, is a man who bores the community with
the details of the illegalities of his private life.

Like most artificial people he had a great love of
nature. " I hold three things in high estimation,"
he says somewhere : " to sit lazily on an eminence
that commands a rich prospect ; to be shadowed by
thick trees while the sun shines around me ; and to
enjoy solitude with the consciousness of neighbourhood. The country gives them all to me." He
writes about his wandering over fragrant furze and
heath repeating Collin's " Ode to Evening," just to
catch the fine quality of the moment ; about smother-
ing his face " in a watery bed of cowslips, wet with
May dews " ; and about the pleasure of seeing the
sweet-breathed kine " pass slowly homeward through
the twilight," and hearing " the distant clank of the
sheep-bell." One phrase of his, " the polyanthus
glowed in its cold bed of earth, like a solitary picture
of Giorgione on a dark oaken panel," is curiously
characteristic of his temperament, and this passage
is rather pretty in its way—

"The short tender grass was covered with marguerites—
'such that men called *daisies* in our town'—thick as stars on
a summer's night. The harsh caw of the busy rooks came

pleasantly mellowed from a high dusky grove of elms at some
distance off, and at intervals was heard the voice of a boy scaring
away the birds from the newly-sown seeds.   The blue depths
were the colour of the darkest ultramarine; not a cloud
streaked the calm æther; only round the horizon's edge
streamed a light, warm film of misty vapour, against which
the near village with its ancient stone church showed sharply
out with blinding whiteness.  I thought of Wordsworth's
' Lines written in March.' "

However, we must not forget that the cultivated
young man who penned these lines, and who was so
susceptible to Wordsworthian influences, was also, as
I said at the beginning of this memoir, one of the
most subtle and secret poisoners of this or any age.
How he first became fascinated by this strange sin
he does not tell us, and the diary in which he carefully noted the results of his terrible experiments and
the methods that he adopted, has unfortunately been
lost to us.   Even in later days, too, he was always
reticent on the matter, and preferred to speak about
" The Excursion," and the " Poems founded on the
Affections."   There is no doubt, however, that the
poison that he used was strychnine.   In one of the
beautiful rings of which he was so proud, and which
served to show off the fine modelling of his delicate
ivory hands, he used to carry crystals of the Indian
*nux vomica*, a poison, one of his biographers tells
us, " nearly tasteless, difficult of discovery, and

capable of almost infinite dilution." His murders, says De Quincey, were more than were ever made known judicially. This is no doubt so, and some of them are worthy of mention. His first victim was his uncle, Mr. Thomas Griffiths. He poisoned him in 1829 to gain possession of Linden House, a place to which he had always been very much attached. In the August of the next year he poisoned Mrs. Abercrombie, his wife's mother, and in the following December he poisoned the lovely Helen Abercrombie, his sister-in-law. Why he murdered Mrs. Abercrombie is not ascertained. It may have been for a caprice, or to quicken some hideous sense of power that was in him, or because she suspected something, or for no reason. But the murder of Helen Abercrombie was carried out by himself and his wife for the sake of a sum of about 18,000*l.* for which they had insured her life in various offices. The circumstances were as follows. On the 12th of December, he and his wife and child came up to London from Linden House, and took lodgings at No. 12, Conduit Street, Regent Street. With them were the two sisters, Helen and Madeleine Abercrombie. On the evening of the 14th they all went to the play, and at supper that night Helen sickened. The next day she was extremely ill, and Dr. Locock, of Hanover Square, was called in to attend her. She lived till Monday, the 20th, when, after the doctor's morning visit, Mr. and Mrs. Wainewright, brought her some poisoned jelly, and then went out for a walk. When they returned Helen Abercrombie was dead. She was about twenty years of age, a tall graceful girl with fair hair. A very charming red-chalk drawing of her by her brother-in-law is still in existence, and shows how much his style as an artist was influenced by Sir Thomas Lawrence, a painter for whose work he had always entertained a great admiration. De Quincey says that Mrs. Wainewright was not really privy to the murder. Let us hope that she was not. Sin should be solitary, and have no accomplices.

The insurance companies, suspecting the real facts of the case, declined to pay the policy on the technical ground of misrepresentation and want of interest, and, with curious courage, the poisoner entered an action in the Court of Chancery against the Imperial, it being agreed that one decision should govern all the cases. The trial, however, did not come on for five years, when, after one disagreement, a verdict was ultimately given in the companies' favour. The judge on the occasion was Lord Abinger. *Egomet Bonmot* was represented by Mr. Erle and Sir William Follet, and the Attorney-General and Sir Frederick Pollock appeared for the other side. The plaintiff, unfortunately, was unable to be

present at either of the trials. The refusal of the
companies to give him the 18,000*l.* had placed him
in a position of most painful pecuniary embarrass-
ment. Indeed, a few months after the murder of
Helen Abercrombie, he had been actually arrested
for debt in the streets of London while he was sere-
nading the pretty daughter of one of his friends.
This difficulty was got over at the time, but shortly
afterwards he thought it better to go abroad till he
could come to some practical arrangement with his
creditors. He accordingly went to Boulogne on a
visit to the father of the young lady in question, and
while he was there induced him to insure his life with
the Pelican Company for 3000*l.* As soon as the necessary formalities had been gone through and the
policy executed, he dropped some crystals of strychnine into his coffee as they sat together one evening
after dinner. He himself did not gain any monetary
advantage by doing this. His aim was simply to re-
venge himself on the first office that had refused to
pay him the price of his sin. His friend died the
next day in his presence, and he left Boulogne at
once for a sketching tour through the most picturesque parts of Brittany, and was for some time the
guest of an old French gentleman, who had a beautiful country house at St. Omer. From this he moved
to Paris, where he remained for several years, living

in luxury, some say, while others talk of his " skulk-
ing with poison in his pockets, and being dreaded
by all who knew him." In 1837 he returned to
England privately. Some strange mad fascination
brought him back. He followed a woman whom he
loved.

It was the month of June, and he was staying at
one of the hotels in Covent Garden. His sitting
room was on the ground floor, and he prudently kept
the blinds down for fear of being seen. Thirteen
years before, when he was making his fine collection
of majolica and Marc Antonios, he had forged the
names of his trustees to a power of attorney, which
enabled him to get possession of some of the money
which he had inherited from his mother, and had
brought into marriage settlement. He knew that
this forgery had been discovered, and that by returning to England he was imperilling his life. Yet he
returned. Should one wonder? It was said that
the woman was very beautiful. Besides, she did
not love him.

It was by a mere accident that he was discovered.
A noise in the street attracted his attention, and, in
his artistic interest in modern life, he pushed aside
the blind for a moment. Some one outside called
out " That's Wainewright, the Bank-forger." It
was Forrester, the Bow Street runner.

On the 5th of July he was brought up at the Old Bailey. The following report of the proceedings appeared in the *Times*:—

"Before Mr. Justice Vaughan and Mr. Baron Alderson, Thomas Griffiths Wainewright, aged forty-two, a man of gentlemanly appearance, wearing mustachios, was indicted for forging and uttering a certain power of attorney for 2259*l*., with intent to defraud the Governor and Company of the Bank of England.

"There were five indictments against the prisoner, to all of which he pleaded not guilty, when he was arraigned before Mr. Serjeant Arabin in the course of the morning. On being brought before the judges, however, he begged to be allowed to withdraw the former plea, and then pleaded guilty to two of the indictments which were not of a capital nature.

"The counsel for the Bank having explained that there were three other indictments, but that the Bank did not desire to shed blood, the plea of guilty on the two minor charges was recorded, and the prisoner at the close of the session sentenced by the Recorder to transportation for life."

He was taken back to Newgate, preparatory to his removal to the colonies. In a fanciful passage in one of his early essays he had fancied himself "lying in Horsemonger Gaol under sentence of death" for having been unable to resist the temptation of stealing some Marc Antonios from the British Museum in order to complete his collection. The sentence now passed on him was to a man of his culture a form of death. He complained bitterly of it to his friends, and pointed out, with a good deal of reason, some people may fancy, that the money was practically his own, having come to him from his mother, and that the forgery, such as it was, had been committed thirteen years before, which to use his own phrase, was at least a *circonstance atténuante*. The permanence of personality is a very subtle metaphysical problem, and certainly the English law solves the question in an extremely rough-and-ready manner. There is, however, something dramatic in the fact that this heavy punishment was inflicted on him for what, if we remember his fatal influence on the prose of modern journalism, was certainly not the worst of all his sins.

While he was in gaol, Dickens, Macready, and Hablot Browne came across him by chance. They had been going over the prisons of London, searching for artistic effects, and in Newgate they suddenly caught sight of Wainewright. He met them with a defiant stare, Forster tells us, but Macready was "horrified to recognize a man familiarly known to him in former years, and at whose table he had dined."

Others had more curiosity, and his cell was for some time a kind of fashionable lounge. Many men of letters went down to visit their old literary comrade. But he was no longer the kind light-hearted Janus whom Charles Lamb admired. He seems to have grown quite cynical.

To the agent of an insurance company who was visiting him one afternoon, and thought he would improve the occasion by pointing out that, after all crime was a bad speculation, he replied: " Sir, you City men enter on your speculations and take the chances of them. Some of your speculations succeed, some fail. Mine happen to have failed, yours happen to have succeeded. That is the only difference, sir, between my visitor and me. But, sir, I will tell you one thing in which I have succeeded, to the last. I have been determined through life to hold the position of a gentleman. I have always done so. I do so still. It is the custom of this place that each of the inmates of a cell shall take his morning's turn of sweeping it out. I occupy a cell with a bricklayer and a sweep, but they never offer me the broom!" When a friend reproached him with the murder of Helen Abercrombie he shrugged his shoulders and said, "Yes; it was a dreadful thing to do, but she had very thick ankles."

From Newgate he was brought to the hulks at Portsmouth, and sent from there in the *Susan* to Van Diemen's Land along with three hundred other convicts. The voyage seems to have been most distasteful to him, and in a letter written to a friend he spoke bitterly about the ignominy of " the companion of poets and artists " being compelled to associate with " country bumpkins." The phrase that he applies to his companions need not surprise us. Crime in England is rarely the result of sin. It is nearly always the result of starvation. There was probably no one on board in whom he would have found a sympathetic listener, or even a psychologically interesting nature.

His love of art, however, never deserted him. At Hobart Town he started a studio, and returned to sketching and portrait-painting, and his conversation and manners seem not to have lost their charm. Nor did he give up his habit of poisoning, and there are two cases on record in which he tried to make away with people who had offended him. But his hand seems to have lost its cunning. Both of his attempts were complete failures, and in 1844, being thoroughly dissatisfied with Tasmanian society, he presented a memorial to the governor of the settlement, Sir John Eardley Wilmot, praying for a ticket-of-leave. In it he speaks of himself as being " tormented by ideas struggling for outward form and realization, barred up from increase of knowledge, and deprived of the exercise of profitable or even of decorous speech." His request, however, was refused, and the associate of Coleridge consoled himself by making those marvellous *Paradis Artificiels* whose secret is only known to the eaters of opium. In 1852 he died of apoplexy, his sole living companion being a cat, for which he had evinced an extraordinary affection.

His crimes seem to have had an important effect upon his art. They gave a strong personality to his style, a quality that his early work certainly lacked. In a note to the Life of Dickens, Forster mentions that in 1847 Lady Blessington received from her brother, Major Power, who held a military appointmeut at Hobart Town, an oil portrait of a young lady from his clever brush; and it is said that " he had contrived to put the expression of his own wickedness into the portrait of a nice, kind-hearted girl." M. Zola, in one of his novels, tells us of a young man who, having committed a murder, takes to art, and paints greenish impressionist portraits of perfectly respectable people, all of which bear a curious resemblance to his victim. The development of Mr. Wainewright's style seems to me far more subtle and suggestive. One can fancy an intense personality being created out of sin.

This strange and fascinating figure that for a few years dazzled literary London, and made so brilliant a *début* in life and letters, is undoubtedly a most interesting study. Mr. W. Carew Hazlitt, his latest biographer, to whom I am indebted for many of the

facts contained in this memoir, and whose little
book is, indeed, quite invaluable in its way, is of
opinion that his love of art and nature was a mere
pretence and assumption, and others have denied to
him all literary power. This seems to me a shallow,
or at least a mistaken, view. The fact of a man being a poisoner is nothing against his prose. The
domestic virtues are not the true basis of art,
though they may serve as an excellent advertisement for second-rate artists. It is possible that De
Quincey exaggerated his critical powers, and I cannot help saying again that there is much in his
published works that is too familiar, too common,
too journalistic, in the bad sense of that bad word.
Here and there he is distinctly vulgar in expression,
and he is always lacking in the self-restraint of the
true artist. But for some of his faults we must
blame the time in which he lived, and, after all,
prose that Charles Lamb thought "capital" has no
small historic interest. That he had a sincere love
of art and nature seems to me quite certain. There
is no essential incongruity between crime and culture. We cannot re-write the whole of history for
the purpose of gratifying our moral sense of what
should be.

Of course, he is far too close to our own time for
us to be able to form any purely artistic judgment

about him. It is impossible not to feel a strong prejudice against a man who might have poisoned Lord Tennyson, or Mr. Gladstone, or the Master of Balliol. But had the man worn a costume and spoken a language different from our own, had he lived in imperial Rome, or at the time of the Italian Renaissance, or in Spain in the seventeenth century, or in any land or any century but this century and this land, we would be quite able to arrive at a perfectly unprejudiced estimate of his position and value. I know that there are many historians, or at least writers on historical subjects, who still think it necessary to apply moral judgments to history, and who distribute their praise or blame with the solemn complacency of a successful schoolmaster. This, however, is a foolish habit, and merely shows that the moral instinct can be brought to such a pitch of perfection that it will make its appearance wherever it is not required. Nobody with the true historical sense ever dreams of blaming Nero, or scolding Tiberius or censuring Cæsar Borgia. These personages have become like the puppets of a play. They may fill us with terror, or horror, or wonder, but they do not harm us. They are not in immediate relation to us. We have nothing to fear from them. They have passed into the sphere of art and science, and neither art

nor science knows anything of moral approval or
disapproval. And so it may be some day with
Charles Lamb's friend. At present I feel that he
is just a little too modern to be treated in that fine
spirit of disinterested curiosity to which we owe so
many charming studies of the great criminals of the
Italian Renaissance from the pens of Mr. John Add-
ington Symonds, Miss A. Mary F. Robinson, Miss
Vernon Lee, and other distinguished writers. However, Art has not forgotten him. He is the hero of
Dickens's *Hunted Down*, the Varney of Bulwer's
*Lucretia;* and it is gratifying to note that fiction
has paid some homage to one who was so powerful with " pen, pencil, and poison." To be suggestive for fiction is to be of more importance than a
fact.

# THE CRITIC AS ARTIST

## WITH SOME REMARKS UPON THE
## IMPORTANCE OF DOING NOTHING

¶ *A DIALOGUE.* *Part I.*
*Persons: Gilbert and Ernest.*
*Scene: the library of a house*
*in Piccadilly, overlooking the*
*Green Park.*

# THE CRITIC AS ARTIST

*Gilbert* (*at the Piano*). My dear Ernest, what are you laughing at?

*Ernest* (*looking up*). At a capital story that I have just come across in this volume of Reminiscences that I have found on your table.

*Gilbert.* What is the book? Ah! I see. I have not read it yet. Is it good?

*Ernest.* Well, while you have been playing, I have been turning over the pages with some amusement, though, as a rule, I dislike modern memoirs. They are generally written by people who have either entirely lost their memories, or have never done anything worth remembering; which, however, is, no doubt, the true explanation of their popularity, as the English public always feels perfectly at its ease when a mediocrity is talking to it.

*Gilbert.* Yes: the public is wonderfully tolerant. It forgives everything except genius. But I must

confess that I like all memoirs.　I like them for their
form, just as much as for their matter.　In literature
mere egotism is delightful.　It is what fascinates us
in the letters of personalities so different as Cicero
and Balzac, Flaubert and Berlioz, Byron and Ma-
dame de Sévigné.　Whenever we come across it, and,
strangely enough, it is rather rare, we cannot but wel-
come it, and do not easily forget it.　Humanity will
always love Rousseau for having confessed his sins,
not to a priest, but to the world, and the couchant
nymphs that Cellini wrought in bronze for the castle
of King Francis, the green and gold Perseus, even,
that in the open Loggia at Florence shows the moon
the dead terror that once turned life to stone, have
not given it more pleasure than has that autobiography in which the supreme scoundrel of the Renaissance relates the story of his splendour and his
shame.　The opinions, the character, the achievements of the man, matter very little.　He may be a
sceptic like the gentle Sieur de Montaigne, or a saint
like the bitter son of Monica, but when he tells us
his own secrets he can always charm our ears to listening and our lips to silence.　The mode of thought
that Cardinal Newman represented—if that can be
called a mode of thought which seeks to solve intellectual problems by a denial of the supremacy of
the intellect—may not, cannot, I think, survive.　But

the world will never weary of watching that troubled
soul in its progress from darkness to darkness.   The
lonely church at Littlemore, where "the breath of
the morning is damp, and worshippers are few," will
always be dear to it, and whenever men see the yellow snapdragon blossoming on the wall of Trinity
they will think of that gracious undergraduate who
saw in the flower's sure recurrence a prophecy that
he would abide for ever with the Benign Mother of
his days—a prophecy that Faith, in her wisdom or
her folly, suffered not to be fulfilled.   Yes; autobiography is irresistible.   Poor, silly, conceited Mr.
Secretary Pepys has chattered his way into the circle
of the Immortals, and, conscious that indiscretion
is the better part of valour, bustles about among
them in that "shaggy purple gown with gold but-
tons and looped lace" which he is so fond of describ-
ing to us, perfectly at his ease, and prattling, to his
own and our infinite pleasure, of the Indian blue pet-
ticoat that he bought for his wife, of the "good
hog's harslet," and the "pleasant French fricassee of
veal" that he loved to eat, of his game of bowls with
Will Joyce, and his "gadding after beauties," and
his reciting of *Hamlet* on a Sunday, and his playing
of the viol on week days, and other wicked or trivial
things.   Even in actual life egotism is not without
its attractions.   When people talk to us about others

they are usually dull.   When they talk to us about
themselves they are nearly always interesting, and
if one could shut them up, when they become wearisome, as easily as one can shut up a book of which
one has grown weary, they would be perfect absolutely.

*Ernest.* There is much virtue in that If, as Touchstone would say.   But do you seriously propose that
every man should become his own Boswell?   What
would become of our industrious compilers of Lives
and Recollections in that case?

*Gilbert.* What has become of them?   They are
the pest of the age, nothing more and nothing less.
Every great man nowadays has his disciples, and
it is always Judas who writes the biography.

*Ernest.* My dear fellow!

*Gilbert.* I am afraid it is true.   Formerly we used
to canonize our heroes.   The modern method is to
vulgarize them.   Cheap editions of great books may
be delightful, but cheap editions of great men are
absolutely detestable.

*Ernest.* May I ask, Gilbert, to whom you allude?

*Gilbert.* Oh! to all our second-rate *litterateurs*.
We are overrun by a set of people who, when poet or
painter passes away, arrive at the house along with
the undertaker, and forget that their one duty is to
behave as mutes.   But we won't talk about them.

They are the mere body-snatchers of literature. The dust is given to one, and the ashes to another, and the soul is out of their reach. And now, let me play Chopin to you, or Dvorák? Shall I play you a fantasy by Dvorák? He writes passionate, curiously-coloured things.

*Ernest.* No; I don't want music just at present. It is far too indefinite. Besides, I took the Baroness Bernstein down to dinner last night, and, though absolutely charming in every other respect, she insisted on discussing music as if it were actually written in the German language. Now, whatever music sounds like, I am glad to say that it does not sound in the smallest degree like German. There are forms of patriotism that are really quite degrading. No; Gilbert, don't play any more. Turn round and talk to me. Talk to me till the white-horned day comes into the room. There is something in your voice that is wonderful.

*Gilbert* (*rising from the piano*). I am not in a mood for talking to-night. How horrid of you to smile? I really am not. Where are the cigarettes? Thanks. How exquisite these single daffodils are! They seem to be made of amber and cool ivory. They are like Greek things of the best period. What was the story in the confessions of the remorseful Academician that made you laugh? Tell it to me.

After playing Chopin, I feel as if I had been weeping over sins that I had never committed, and mourning over tragedies that were not my own. Music always seems to me to produce that effect. It creates for one a past of which one has been ignorant, and fills one with a sense of sorrows that have been hidden from one's tears. I can fancy a man who had led a perfectly commonplace life, hearing by chance some curious piece of music, and suddenly discovering that his soul, without his being conscious of it, had passed through terrible experiences, and known fearful joys, or wild romantic loves, or great renunciations. And so, tell me this story, Ernest. I want to be amused.

*Ernest.* Oh! I don't know that it is of any importance. But I thought it a really admirable illustration of the true value of ordinary art-criticism. It seems that a lady once gravely asked the remorseful Academician, as you call him, if his celebrated picture of "A Spring-Day at Whiteley's," or "Waiting for the Last Omnibus," or some subject of that kind, was all painted by hand?

*Gilbert.* And was it?

*Ernest.* You are quite incorrigible. But, seriously speaking, what is the use of art-criticism? Why cannot the artist be left alone, to create a new world if he wishes it, or, if not, to shadow forth the world which we already know, and of which, I fancy, we would each one of us be wearied if Art, with her fine spirit of choice and delicate instinct of selection, did not, as it were, purify it for us, and give to it a momentary perfection. It seems to me that the imagination spreads, or should spread, a solitude around it, and works best in silence and in isolation. Why should the artist be troubled by the shrill clamour of criticism? Why should those who cannot create take upon themselves to estimate the value of creative work? What can they know about it? If a man's work is easy to understand, an explanation is unnecessary. . . .

*Gilbert.* And if his work is incomprehensible, an explanation is wicked.

*Ernest.* I did not say that.

*Gilbert.* Ah! but you should have. Nowadays, we have so few mysteries left to us that we cannot afford to part with one of them. The members of the Browning Society, like the theologians of the Broad Church Party, or the authors of Mr. Walter Scott's Great Writers' Series, seem to me to spend their time in trying to explain their divinity away. Where one had hoped that Browning was a mystic, they have sought to show that he was simply inarticulate. Where one had fancied that he had something to conceal, they have proved that he had

but little to reveal.  But I speak merely of his incoherent work.  Taken as a whole, the man was
great.  He did not belong to the Olympians, and
had all the incompleteness of the Titan.  He did not
survey, and it was but rarely that he could sing.
His work is marred by struggle, violence and effort,
and he passed not from emotion to form, but from
thought to chaos.  Still, he was great.  He has
been called a thinker, and was certainly a man who
was always thinking, and always thinking aloud;
but it was not thought that fascinated him, but
rather the processes by which thought moves.  It was
the machine he loved, not what the machine makes.
The method by which the fool arrives at his folly
was as dear to him as the ultimate wisdom of the
wise.  So much, indeed, did the subtle mechanism
of mind fascinate him that he despised language, or
looked upon it as an incomplete instrument of expression.  Rhyme, that exquisite echo which in the
Muse's hollow hill creates and answers its own
voice; rhyme, which in the hands of the real artist
becomes not merely a material element of metrical
beauty, but a spiritual element of thought and passion also, waking a new mood, it may be, or stirring
a fresh train of ideas, or opening by mere sweetness
and suggestion of sound some golden door at which
the Imagination itself had knocked in vain; rhyme,

which can turn man's utterance to the speech of
gods; rhyme, the one chord we have added to the
Greek lyre, became in Robert Browning's hands a
grotesque, misshapen thing, which made him at
times masquerade in poetry as a low comedian, and
ride Pegasus too often with his tongue in his cheek.
There are moments when he wounds us by monstrous music.   Nay, if he can only get his music by
breaking the strings of his lute, he breaks them, and
they snap in discord, and no Athenian tettix, making
melody from tremulous wings, lights on the ivory
horn to make the movement perfect, or the interval
less harsh.   Yet, he was great: and though he
turned language into ignoble clay, he made from it
men and women that live.   He is the most Shakes-
perian creature since Shakespeare.   If Shakespeare
could sing with myriad lips, Browning could. stam-
mer through a thousand mouths.   Even now, as I
am speaking, and speaking not against him but for
him, there glides through the room the pageant of
his persons.   There, creeps Fra Lippo Lippi with
his cheeks still burning from some girl's hot kiss.
There, stands dread Saul with the lordly male-
sapphires gleaming in his turban.   Mildred Tresham
is there, and the Spanish monk, yellow with hatred,
and Blougram, and Ben Ezra, and the Bishop of
St. Praxed's.   The spawn of Setebos gibbers in the

corner, and Sebald, hearing Pippa pass by, looks
on Ottima's haggard face, and loathes her and his
own sin, and himself.    Pale as the white satin of his
doublet, the melancholy king watches with dreamy
treacherous eyes too loyal Strafford pass forth to his
doom, and Andrea shudders as he hears the cousin's
whistle in the garden, and bids his perfect wife go
down.    Yes, Browning was great.    And as what will
he be remembered?  As a poet?  Ah, not as a poet!
He will be remembered as a writer of fiction, as the
most supreme writer of fiction, it may be, that we
have ever had.    His sense of dramatic situation was
unrivalled, and, if he could not answer his own problems, he could at least put problems forth, and what
more should an artist do?  Considered from the
point of view of a creator of character he ranks next
to him who made Hamlet.  Had he been articulate, he
might have sat beside him.    The only man who can
touch the hem of his garment is George Meredith.
Meredith is a prose Browning, and so is Browning.
He used poetry as a medium for writing in prose.

*Ernest.* There is something in what you say, but
there is not everything in what you say.   In many
points you are unjust.

*Gilbert.* It is difficult not to be unjust to what one
loves.    But let us return to the particular point at
issue.    What was it that you said?

*Ernest.* Simply this: that in the best days of art there were no art-critics.

*Gilbert.* I seem to have heard that observation before, Ernest. It has all the vitality of error and all the tediousness of an old friend.

*Ernest.* It is true. Yes: there is no use your tossing your head in that petulant manner. It is quite true. In the best days of art there were no art-critics. The sculptor hewed from the marble block the great white-limbed Hermes that slept within it. The waxers and gilders of images gave tone and texture to the statue, and the world, when it saw it, worshipped and was dumb. He poured the glowing bronze into the mould of sand, and the river of red metal cooled into noble curves and took the impress of the body of a god. With enamel or polished jewels he gave sight to the sightless eyes. The hyacinth-like curls grew crisp beneath his graver. And when, in some dim frescoed fane, or pillared sunlit portico, the child of Leto stood upon his pedestal, those who passed by, ἀβρῶς βαίνοντες διὰ λαμπροτάτου αἰθέρος, became conscious of a new influence that had come across their lives, and dreamily, or with a sense of strange and quickening joy, went to their homes or daily labour, or wandered, it may be, through the city gates to that nymph-haunted meadow where young Phædrus bathed his feet, and, lying there on the soft grass, beneath the tall wind-whispering planes and flowering *agnus castus*, began to think of the wonder of beauty, and grew silent with unaccustomed awe. In those days the artist was free. From the river valley he took the fine clay in his fingers, and with a little tool of wood or bone, fashioned it into forms so exquisite that the people gave them to the dead as their playthings, and we find them still in the dusty tombs on the yellow hillside by Tanagra, with the faint gold and the fading crimson still lingering about hair and lips and raiment. On a wall of fresh plaster, stained with bright sandyx or mixed with milk and saffron, he pictured one who trod with tired feet the purple white-starred fields of asphodel, one 'in whose eyelids lay the whole of the Trojan War,' Polyxena, the daughter of Priam; or figured Odysseus, the wise and cunning, bound by tight cords to the mast-step, that he might listen without hurt to the singing of the Sirens, or wandering by the clear river of Acheron, where the ghosts of fishes flitted over the pebbly bed; or showed the Persian in trews and mitre flying before the Greek at Marathon, or the galleys clashing their beaks of brass in the little Salaminian bay. He drew with silver-point and charcoal upon parchment and prepared cedar. Upon ivory and rose-coloured terra-cotta he painted with wax, making the wax fluid with juice of olives, and with heated irons making it firm. Panel and marble and linen canvas became wonderful as his brush swept across them; and life, seeing her own image, was still, and dared not speak. All life, indeed, was his, from the merchants seated in the market-place to the cloaked shepherd lying on the hill; from the nymph hidden in the laurels and the faun that piped at noon, to the king whom, in long green-curtained litter, slaves bore upon oil-bright shoulders, and fanned with peacock fans. Men and women, with pleasure or sorrow in their faces, passed before him. He watched them, and their secret became his. Through form and colour he re-created a world.

All subtle arts belonged to him also. He held the gem against the revolving disk, and the amethyst became the purple couch for Adonis, and across the veined sardonyx sped Artemis with her hounds. He beat out the gold into roses, and strung them to-gether for necklace or armlet. He beat out the gold into wreaths for the conqueror's helmet, or into palmates for the Tyrian robe, or into masks for the royal dead. On the back of the silver mirror he graved Thetis borne by her Nereids, or love-sick Phædra with her nurse, or Persephone, weary of memory, putting poppies in her hair. The potter

sat in his shed, and, flower-like from the silent
wheel, the vase rose up beneath his hands. He
decorated the base and stem and ears with pattern
of dainty olive-leaf, or foliated acanthus, or curved
and crested wave. Then in black or red he painted
lads wrestling, or in the race: knights in full
armour, with strange heraldic shields and çurious
visors, leaning from shell-shaped chariot over rear-
ing steeds: the gods seated at the feast or working
their miracles: the heroes in their victory or in their
pain. Sometimes he would etch in thin vermilion
lines upon a ground of white the languid bridegroom
and his bride, with Eros hovering round them—an
Eros like one of Donatello's angels, a little laughing
thing with gilded or with azure wings. On the
curved side he would write the name of his friend.
ΚΑΛΟΣ ΑΛΚΙΒΙΑΔΗΣ or ΚΑΛΟΣ ΧΑΡΜΙΔΗΣ tells
us the story of his days. Again, on the rim of the
wide flat cup he would draw the stag browsing, or
the lion at rest, as his fancy willed it. From the
tiny perfume-bottle laughed Aphrodite at her toilet
and, with bare-limbed Mænads in his train, Diony-
sus danced round the wine-jar on naked must-
stained feet, while, satyr-like, the old Silenus
sprawled upon the bloated skins, or shook that
magic spear which was tipped with a fretted fir-
cone, and wreathed with dark ivy. And no one

came to trouble the artist at his work. No irresponsible chatter disturbed him. He was not worried by opinions. By the Ilyssus, says Arnold somewhere, there was no Higginbotham. By the Ilyssus, my dear Gilbert, there were no silly art-congresses, bringing provincialism to the provinces and teaching the mediocrity how to mouth. By the Ilyssus there were no tedious magazines about art, in which the industrious prattle of what they do not understand. On the reed-grown banks of that little stream strutted no ridiculous journalism monopolizing the seat of judgment when it should be apologizing in the dock. The Greeks had no art-critics.

*Gilbert.* Ernest, you are quite delightful, but your views are terribly unsound. I am afraid that you have been listening to the conversation of someone older than yourself. That is always a dangerous thing to do, and if you allow it to degenerate into a habit, you will find it absolutely fatal to any intellectual development. As for modern journalism, it is not my business to defend it. It justifies its own existence by the great Darwinian principle of the survival of the vulgarest. I have merely to do with literature.

*Ernest.* But what is the difference between literature and journalism?

*Gilbert.* Oh! journalism is unreadable, and literature is not read. That is all. But with regard to your statement that the Greeks had no art-critics, I assure you that is quite absurd. It would be more just to say that the Greeks were a nation of art-critics.

*Ernest.* Really?

*Gilbert.* Yes, a nation of art-critics. But I don't wish to destroy the delightfully unreal picture that you have drawn of the relation of the Hellenic artist to the intellectual spirit of his age. To give an accurate description of what has never occurred is not merely the proper occupation of the historian, but the inalienable privilege of any man of parts and culture. Still less do I desire to talk learnedly. Learned conversation is either the affectation of the ignorant or the profession of the mentally unemployed. And as for what is called improving conversation, that is merely the foolish method by which the still more foolish philanthropist feebly tries to disarm the just rancour of the criminal classes. No: let me play to you some mad scarlet thing by Dvorák. The pallid figures on the tapestry are smiling at us, and the heavy eyelids of my bronze Narcissus are folded in sleep. Don't let us discuss anything solemnly. I am but too conscious of the fact that we are born in an age when only the dull are treated seriously, and I live in terror of not being misunderstood. Don't degrade me into the position of giving you useful information. Education is an admirable thing, but it is well to remember from time to time that nothing that is worth knowing can be taught. Through the parted curtains of the window I see the moon like a clipped piece of silver. Like gilded bees the stars cluster round her. The sky is a hard hollow sapphire. Let us go out into the night. Thought is wonderful, but adventure is more wonderful still. Who knows but we may meet Prince Florizel of Bohemia, and hear the fair Cuban tell us that she is not what she seems?

*Ernest.* You are horribly wilful. I insist on your discussing this matter with me. You have said that the Greeks were a nation of art-critics. What art-criticism have they left us?

*Gilbert.* My dear Ernest, even if not a single fragment of art-criticism had come down to us from Hellenic or Hellenistic days, it would be none the less true that the Greeks were a nation of art-critics, and that they invented the criticism of art just as they invented the criticism of everything else. For, after all, what is our primary debt to the Greeks? Simply the critical spirit. And, this spirit, which they exercised on questions of religion

and science, of ethics and metaphysics, of politics
and education, they exercised on questions of art
also, and, indeed, of the two supreme and highest
arts, they have left us the most flawless system of
criticism that the world has ever seen.

*Ernest.* But what are the two supreme and highest arts?

*Gilbert.* Life and Literature, life and the perfect
expression of life. The principles of the former, as
laid down by the Greeks, we may not realize in an
age so marred by false ideals as our own. The
principles of the latter, as they laid them down, are,
in many cases, so subtle that we can hardly understand them. Recognizing that the most perfect art is
that which most fully mirrors man in all his infinite
variety, they elaborated the criticism of language,
considered in the light of the mere material of that
art, to a point to which we, with our accentual system of reasonable or emotional emphasis, can barely
if at all attain; studying, for instance, the metrical
movements of a prose as scientifically as a modern
musician studies harmony and counterpoint, and, I
need hardly say, with much keener æsthetic instinct.
In this they were right, as they were right in all
things. Since the introduction of printing, and the
fatal development of the habit of reading amongst
the middle and lower classes of this country, there

has been a tendency in literature to appeal more and
more to the eye, and less and less to the ear, which
is really the sense which, from the standpoint of
pure art, it should seek to please, and by whose
canons of pleasure it should abide always.   Even the
work of Mr. Pater, who is, on the whole, the most
perfect master of English prose now creating amongst
us, is often far more like a piece of mosaic than a
passage in music, and seems, here and there, to lack
the true rhythmical life of words and the fine freedom and richness of effect that such rhythmical life
produces.   We, in fact, have made writing a definite
mode of composition, and have treated it as a form
of elaborate design.   The Greeks, upon the other
hand, regarded writing simply as a method of chronicling.   Their test was always the spoken word in
its musical and metrical relations.   The voice was
the medium, and the ear the critic.   I have sometimes thought that the story of Homer's blindness
might be really an artistic myth, created in critical
days, and serving to remind us, not merely that the
great poet is always a seer, seeing less with the
eyes of the body than he does with the eyes of the
soul, but that he is a true singer also, building his
song out of music, repeating each line over and
over again to himself till he has caught the secret
of its melody, chaunting in darkness the words that

are winged with light.   Certainly, whether this be
so or not, it was to his blindness, as an occasion if
not as a cause, that England's great poet owed
much of the majestic movement and sonorous splendour of 'his later verse.   When Milton could no
longer write, he began to sing.   Who would match
the measures of *Comus* with the measures of *Sam-
son Agonistes*, or of *Paradise Lost* or *Regained?*
When Milton became blind he composed, as every-
one should compose, with the voice purely, and so
the pipe or reed of earlier days became that mighty
many-stopped organ whose rich reverberant music
has all the stateliness of Homeric verse, if it seeks
not to have its swiftness, and is the one imperish-
able inheritance of English literature, sweeping
through all the ages, because above them, and
abiding with us ever, being immortal in its form.
Yes: writing has done much harm to writers.
We must return to the voice.   That must be our
test, and perhaps then we shall be able to appreciate
some of the subtleties of Greek art-criticism.

   As it now is, we cannot do so.   Sometimes, when
I have written a piece of prose that I have been
modest enough to consider absolutely free from
fault, a dreadful thought comes over me that I
may have been guilty of the immoral effeminacy of
using trochaic and tribrachic movements, a crime

for which a learned critic of the Augustan age
censures with most just severity the brilliant if
somewhat paradoxical Hegesias.    I grow cold when
I think of it, and wonder to myself if the admirable
ethical effect of the prose of that charming writer,
who once in a spirit of reckless generosity towards
the uncultivated portion of our community pro-
claimed the monstrous doctrine that conduct is
three-fourths of life, will not some day be entirely
annihilated by the discovery that the pæons have
been wrongly placed.

    *Ernest.* Ah! now you are flippant.

    *Gilbert.* Who would not be flippant when he is
gravely told that the Greeks had no art-critics?    I
can understand it being said that the constructive
genius of the Greeks lost itself in criticism, but not
that the race to whom we owe the critical spirit did
not criticise.    You will not ask me to give you a survey of Greek art-criticism from Plato to Plotinus.
The night is too lovely for that, and the moon, if she
heard us, would put more ashes on her face than are
there already.    But think merely of one perfect little
work of æsthetic criticism, Aristotle's *Treatise on
Poetry*.    It is not perfect in form, for it is badly written, consisting perhaps of notes jotted down for an
art lecture, or of isolated fragments destined for
some larger book, but in temper and treatment it is

perfect absolutely. The ethical effect of art, its importance to culture, and its place in the formation of character, had been done once for all by Plato; but here we have art treated, not from the moral, but from the purely æsthetic point of view. Plato had, of course, dealt with many definitely artistic subjects, such as the importance of unity in a work of art, the necessity for tone and harmony, the æsthetic value of appearances, the relation of the visible arts to the external world, and the relation of fiction to fact. He first perhaps stirred in the soul of man that desire which we have not yet satisfied, the desire to know the connection between Beauty and Truth, and the place of Beauty in the moral and intellectual order of the Kosmos. The problems of idealism and realism, as he sets them forth, may seem to many to be somewhat barren of result in the metaphysical sphere of abstract being in which he places them, but transfer them to the sphere of art, and you will find that they are still vital and full of meaning. It may be that it is as a critic of Beauty that Plato is destined to live, and that by altering the name of the sphere of his speculation we shall find a new philosophy. But Aristotle, like Goethe, deals with art primarily in its concrete manifestations, taking Tragedy, for instance, and investigating the material it uses, which is language, its subject-matter, which is life, the method by which it works, which is action, the conditions under which it reveals itself, which are those of theatric presentation, its logical structure, which is plot, and its final æsthetic appeal, which is to the sense of beauty realized through the passions of pity and awe. That purification and spiritualizing of the nature which he calls κάθαρσις is, as Goethe saw, essentially æsthetic, and is not moral, as Lessing fancied. Concerning himself primarily with the impression that the work of art produces, Aristotle sets himself to analyse that impression, to investigate its source, to see how it is engendered. As a physiologist and psychologist, he knows that the health of a function resides in energy. To have a capacity for a passion and not to realize it, is to make oneself incomplete and limited. The mimic spectacle of life that Tragedy affords cleanses the bosom of much 'perilous stuff,' and by presenting high and worthy objects for the exercise of the emotions purifies and spiritualizes the man; nay, not merely does it spiritualize him, but it initiates him also into noble feelings of which he might else have known nothing, the word κάθαρσις having, it has sometimes seemed to me, a definite allusion to the rite of initiation, if indeed that be not, as I am occasionally tempted to fancy, its true and only meaning here. This is of course a mere outline of the book.

But you see what a perfect piece of æsthetic criticism it is.   Who indeed but a Greek could have
analysed art so well?   After reading it, one does not
wonder any longer that Alexandria devoted itself
so largely to art-criticism, and that we find the artistic temperaments of the day investigating every
question of style and manner, discussing the great
Academic schools of painting, for instance, such as
the school of Sicyon, that sought to preserve the
dignified traditions of the antique mode, or the
realistic and impressionist schools, that aimed at re-
producing actual life, or the elements of ideality in
portraiture, or the artistic value of the epic form in
an age so modern as theirs, or the proper subject-
matter for the artist.   Indeed, I fear that the inartistic temperaments of the day busied themselves also
in matters of literature and art, for the accusations
of plagiarism were endless, and such accusations proceed either from the thin colourless lips of impo-
tence, or from the grotesque mouths of those who,
possessing nothing of their own, fancy that they can
gain a reputation for wealth by crying out that they
have been robbed.   And I assure you, my dear Ernest, that the Greeks chattered about painters quite
as much as people do nowadays, and had their private
views, and shilling exhibitions, and Arts and Crafts
guilds, and Pre-Raphael movements, and movements

towards realism, and lectured about art, and wrote essays on art, and produced their art-historians, and their archæologists, and all the rest of it. Why, even the theatrical managers of travelling companies brought their dramatic critics with them when they went on tour, and paid them very handsome salaries for writing laudatory notices. Whatever, in fact, is modern in our life we owe to the Greeks. Whatever is an anachronism is due to mediævalism. It is the Greeks who have given us the whole system of art-criticism, and how fine their critical instinct was, may be seen from the fact that the material they criticised with most care was, as I have already said, language. For the material that painter or sculptor uses is meagre in comparison with that of words. Words have not merely music as sweet as that of viol and lute, colour as rich and vivid as any that makes lovely for us the canvas of the Venetian or the Spaniard, and plastic form no less sure and certain than that which reveals itself in marble or in bronze, but thought and passion and spirituality are theirs also, are theirs indeed alone. If the Greeks had criticised nothing but language, they would still have been the great art-critics of the world. To know the principles of the highest art, is to know the principles of all the arts.

But I see that the moon is hiding behind a sulphur-

coloured cloud.  Out of a tawny mane of drift she
gleams like a lion's eye.  She is afraid that I will talk
to you of Lucian and Longinus, of Quinctilian and
Dionysius, of Pliny and Fronto and Pausanias, of all
those who in the antique world wrote or lectured
upon art-matters.  She need not be afraid.  I am
tired of my expedition into the dim, dull abyss of
facts.  There is nothing left for me now but the
divine μονόχρονος ἡδονή of another cigarette.  Cigarettes have at least the charm of leaving one unsatisfied.

*Ernest.*  Try one of mine.  They are rather good.
I get them direct from Cairo.  The only use of our
*attachés* is that they supply their friends with excellent tobacco.  And as the moon has hidden herself,
let us talk a little longer.  I am quite ready to admit
that I was wrong in what I said about the Greeks.
They were, as you have pointed out, a nation of art-
critics.  I acknowledge it, and I feel a little sorry for
them.  For the creative faculty is higher than the
critical.  There is really no comparison between
them.

*Gilbert.*  The antithesis between them is entirely
arbitrary.  Without the critical faculty, there is no
artistic creation at all, worthy of the name.  You
spoke a little while ago of that fine spirit of choice
and delicate instinct of selection by which the artist

realizes life for us, and gives to it a momentary perfection. Well, that spirit of choice, that subtle tact
of omission, is really the critical faculty in one of its
most characteristic moods, and no one who does not
possess this critical faculty can create anything at
all in art. Arnold's definition of literature as a criticism of life, was not very felicitous in form, but it
showed how keenly he recognized the importance
of the critical element in all creative work.

*Ernest.* I should have said that great artists
worked unconsciously, that they were " wiser than
they knew," as, I think, Emerson remarks somewhere.

*Gilbert.* It is really not so, Ernest. All fine
imaginative work is self-conscious and deliberate.
No poet sings because he must sing. At least, no
great poet does. A great poet sings because he
chooses to sing. It is so now, and it has always been
so. We are sometimes apt to think that the voices
that sounded at the dawn of poetry were simpler,
fresher, and more natural than ours, and that the
world which the early poets looked at, and through
which they walked, had a kind of poetical quality of
its own, and almost without changing could pass into
song. The snow lies thick now upon Olympus, and
its steep scarped sides are bleak and barren, but
once, we fancy, the white feet of the Muses brushed

the dew from the anemones in the morning, and at evening came Apollo to sing to the shepherds in the vale.    But in this we are merely lending to other ages what we desire, or think we desire, for our own. Our historical sense is at fault.    Every century that produces poetry is, so far, an artificial century, and the work that seems to us to be the most natural and simple product of its time is always the result of the most self-conscious effort.    Believe me, Ernest, there is no fine art without self-consciousness, and self-consciousness and the critical spirit are one.

*Ernest.* I see what you mean, and there is much in it.    But surely you would admit that the great poems of the early world, the primitive, anonymous collective poems, were the result of the imagination of races, rather than of the imagination of individuals?

*Gilbert.* Not when they became poetry.    Not when they received a beautiful form.    For there is no art where there is no style, and no style where there is no unity, and unity is of the individual. No doubt Homer had old ballads and stories to deal with, as Shakespeare had chronicles and plays and novels from which to work, but they were merely his rough material.    He took them, and shaped them into song.    They become his, because he made them lovely.    They were built out of music,

" And so not built at all,
And therefore built for ever."

The longer one studies life and literature, the more
strongly one feels that behind everything that is
wonderful stands the individual, and that it is not the
moment that makes the man, but the man who
creates the age.    Indeed, I am inclined to think that
each myth and legend that seems to us to spring out
of the wonder, or terror, or fancy of tribe and nation,
was in its origin the invention of one single mind.
The curiously limited number of the myths seems to
me to point to this conclusion.    But we must not go
off into questions of comparative mythology.    We
must keep to criticism.    And what I want to point
out is this.    An age that has no criticism is either
an age in which art is immobile, hieratic, and confined to the reproduction of formal types, or an age
that possesses no art at all.    There have been
critical ages that have not been creative, in the
ordinary sense of the word, ages in which the spirit
of man has sought to set in order the treasures of
his treasure house, to separate the gold from the
silver, and the silver from the lead, to count over the
jewels, and to give names to the pearls.    But there
has never been a creative age that has not been
critical also.    For it is the critical faculty that invents fresh forms.    The tendency of creation is to

repeat itself.   It is to the critical instinct that we
owe each new school that springs up, each new
mould that art finds ready to its hand.   There is
really not a single form that art now uses that does
not come to us from the critical spirit of Alexandria,
where these forms were either stereotyped, or invented, or made perfect.   I say Alexandria, not
merely beeause it was there that the Greek spirit
became most self-conscious, and indeed ultimately
expired in scepticism and theology, but because it
was to that city, and not to Athens, that Rome
turned for her models, and it was through the
survival, such as it was, of the Latin language that
culture lived at all.   When, at the Renaissance,
Greek literature dawned upon Europe, the soil had
been in some measure prepared for it.   But, to get
rid of the details of history, which are always wearisome and usually inaccurate, let us say generally,
that the forms of art have been due to the Greek
critical spirit.   To it we owe the epic, the lyric, the
entire drama in every one of its developments, including burlesque, the idyll, the romantic novel, the
novel of adventure, the essay, the dialogue, the
oration, the lecture, for which perhaps we should not
forgive them, and the epigram, in all the wide meaning of that word.   In fact, we owe it everything,
except the sonnet, to which, however, some curious

parallels of thought-movement may be traced in the Anthology, American journalism, to which no parallel can be found anywhere, and the ballad in sham Scotch dialect, which one of our most industrious writers has recently proposed should be made the basis for a final and unanimous effort on the part of our second-rate poets to make themselves really romantic. Each new school, as it appears, cries out against criticism, but it is to the critical faculty in man that it owes its origin. The mere creative instinct does not innovate, but reproduces.

*Ernest.* You have been talking of criticism as an essential part of the creative spirit, and I now fully accept your theory. But what of criticism outside creation? I have a foolish habit of reading periodicals, and it seems to me that most modern criticism is perfectly valueless.

*Gilbert.* So is most modern creative work also. Mediocrity weighing mediocrity in the balance, and incompetence applauding its brother—that is the spectacle which the artistic activity of England affords us from time to time. And yet, I feel I am a little unfair in this matter. As a rule, the critics— I speak, of course, of the higher class, of those in fact who write for the sixpenny papers—are far more cultured than the people whose work they are called upon to review. This is, indeed, only what one would expect, for criticism demands infinitely more cultivation than creation does.

*Ernest.* Really?

*Gilbert.* Certainly. Anybody can write a three-volumed novel. It merely requires a complete ignorance of both life and literature. The difficulty that I should fancy the reviewer feels is the difficulty of sustaining any standard. Where there is no style a standard must be impossible. The poor reviewers are apparently reduced to be the reporters of the police-court of literature, the chroniclers of the doings of the habitual criminals of art. It is sometimes said of them that they do not read all through the works they are called upon to criticise. They do not. Or at least they should not. If they did so, they would become confirmed misanthropes, or if I may borrow a phrase from one of the pretty Newnham graduates, confirmed womanthropes for the rest of their lives. Nor is it necessary. To know the vintage and quality of a wine one need not drink the whole cask. It must be perfectly easy in half an hour to say whether a book is worth anything or worth nothing. Ten minutes are really sufficient, if one has the instinct for form. Who wants to wade through a dull volume? One tastes it, and that is quite enough—more than enough, I should imagine. I am aware that there are many

honest workers in painting as well as in literature
who object to criticism entirely. They are quite
right. Their work stands in no intellectual relation
to their age. It brings us no new element of
pleasure. It suggests no fresh departure of thought,
or passion, or beauty. It should not be spoken of.
It should be left to the oblivion that it deserves.

*Ernest.* But, my dear fellow—excuse me for inter-
rupting you—you seem to me to be allowing your
passion for criticism to lead you a great deal too far.
For, after all, even you must admit that it is much
more difficult to do a thing than to talk about it.

*Gilbert.* More difficult to do a thing than to talk
about it? Not at all. That is a gross popular
error. It is very much more difficult to talk about a
thing than to do it. In the sphere of actual life that
is of course obvious. Anybody can make history.
Only a great man can write it. There is no mode
of action, no form of emotion, that we do not share
with the lower animals. It is only by language that
we rise above them, or above each other—by language, which is the parent, and not the child, of
thought. Action, indeed, is always easy, and when
presented to us in its most aggravated, because most
continuous form, which I take to be that of real industry, becomes simply the refuge of people who
have nothing whatsoever to do. No, Ernest, don't

talk about action.   It is a blind thing dependent
on external influences, and moved by an impulse
of whose nature it is unconscious.   It is a thing incomplete in its essence, because limited by accident,
and ignorant of its direction, being always at variance
with its aim.   Its basis is the lack of imagination.
It is the last resource of those who know not how
to dream.

*Ernest*. Gilbert, you treat the world as if it were
a crystal ball.   You hold it in your hand, and reverse
it to please a wilful fancy.   You do nothing but re-
write history.

*Gilbert*. The one duty we owe to history is to re-
write it.   That is not the least of the tasks in store
for the critical spirit.   When we have fully discovered
the scientific laws that govern life, we shall realize
that the one person who has more illusions than the
dreamer is the man of action.   He, indeed, knows
neither the origin of his deeds nor their results.
From the field in which he thought that he had
sown thorns, we have gathered our vintage, and the
fig-tree that he planted for our pleasure is as barren
as the thistle, and more bitter.   It is because
Humanity has never known where it was going that
it has been able to find its way.

*Ernest*. You think, then, that in the sphere of
action a conscious aim is a delusion?

ful than philosophy, as its subject is concrete and not abstract, real and not vague. It is the only civilized form of autobiography, as it deals not with the events, but with the thoughts of one's life; not with life's physical accidents of deed or circumstance, but with the spiritual moods and imaginative passions of the mind. I am always amused by the silly vanity of those writers and artists of our day who seem to imagine that the primary function of the critic is to chatter about their second-rate work. The best that one can say of most modern creative art is that it is just a little less vulgar than reality, and so the critic, with his fine sense of distinction and sure instinct of delicate refinement, will prefer to look into the silver mirror or through the woven veil, and will turn his eyes away from the chaos and clamour of actual existence, though the mirror be tarnished and the veil be torn. His sole aim is to chronicle his own impressions. It is for him that pictures are painted, books written, and marble hewn into form.

*Ernest.* I seem to have heard another theory of Criticism.

*Gilbert.* Yes: it has been said by one whose gracious memory we all revere, and the music of whose pipe once lured Proserpina from her Sicilian fields, and made those white feet stir, and not in vain, the Cumnor cowslips, that the proper aim of Criticism is to see the object as in itself it really is. But this is a very serious error, and takes no cognizance of Criticism's most perfect form, which is in its essence purely subjective, and seeks to reveal its own secret and not the secret of another. For the highest Criticism deals with art not as expressive but as impressive purely.

*Ernest.* But is that really so?

*Gilbert.* Of course it is. Who cares whether Mr. Ruskin's views on Turner are sound or not? What does it matter? That mighty and majestic prose of his, so fervid and so fiery-coloured in its noble eloquence, so rich in its elaborate symphonic music, so sure and certain, at its best, in subtle choice of word and epithet, is at least as great a work of art as any of those wonderful sunsets that bleach or rot on their corrupted canvases in England's Gallery; greater indeed, one is apt to think at times, not merely because its equal beauty is more enduring, but on account of the fuller variety of its appeal, soul speaking to soul in those long-cadenced lines, not through form and colour alone, though through these, indeed, completely and without loss, but with intellectual and emotional utterance, with lofty passion and with loftier thought, with imaginative insight, and with poetic aim; greater, I always think, even as

Literature is the greater art. Who, again, cares whether Mr. Pater has put into the portrait of Monna Lisa something that Lionardo never dreamed of? The painter may have been merely the slave of an archaic smile, as some have fancied, but whenever I pass into the cool galleries of the Palace of the Louvre, and stand before that strange figure " set in its marble chair in that cirque of fantastic rocks, as in some faint light under sea," I murmur to myself, " She is older than the rocks among which she sits; like the vampire, she has been dead many times, and learned the secrets of the grave; and has been a diver in deep seas, and keeps their fallen day about her; and trafficked for strange webs with Eastern merchants; and, as Leda, was the mother of Helen of Troy, and, as St. Anne, the mother of Mary; and all this has been to her but as the sound of lyres and flutes, and lives only in the delicacy with which it has moulded the changing lineaments, and tinged the eyelids and the hands." And I say to my friend, " The presence that thus so strangely rose beside the waters is expressive of what in the ways of a thousand years man had come to desire;" and he answers me, " Hers is the head upon which all 'the ends of the world are come,' and the eyelids are a little weary."

And so the picture becomes more wonderful to us

than it really is, and reveals to us a secret of which, in truth, it knows nothing, and the music of the mystical prose is as sweet in our ears as was that flute-player's music that lent to the lips of La Gioconda those subtle and poisonous curves. Do you ask me what Lionardo would have said had any-one told him of this picture that " all the thoughts and experience of the world had etched and moulded therein that which they had of power to refine and make expressive the outward form, the animalism of Greece, the lust of Rome, the reverie of the Middle Age with its spiritual ambition and imaginative loves, the return of the Pagan world, the sins of the Borgias ? " He would probably have answered that he had contemplated none of these things, but had concerned himself simply with certain arrange-ments of lines and masses, and with new and curious colour-harmonies of blue and green. And it is for this very reason that the criticism which I have quoted is criticism of the highest kind. It treats the work of art simply as a starting point for a new creation. It does not confine itself—let us at least suppose so for the moment—to discovering the real intention of the artist and accepting that as final. And in this it is right, for the meaning of any beauti-ful created thing is, at least, as much in the soul of him who looks at it, as it was in his soul who wrought it. Nay, it is rather the beholder who lends to the beautiful thing its myriad meanings, and makes it marvellous for us, and sets it in some new relation to the age, so that it becomes a vital portion of our lives, and a symbol of what we pray for, or perhaps of what, having prayed for, we fear that we may receive. The longer I study, Ernest, the more clearly I see that the beauty of the visible arts is, as the beauty of music, impressive primarily, and that it may be marred, and indeed often is so, by any excess of intellectual intention on the part of the artist. For when the work is finished it has, as it were, an independent life of its own, and may deliver a message far other than that which was put into its lips to say. Sometimes, when I listen to the overture to *Tannhäuser*, I seem indeed to see that comely knight treading delicately on the flower-strewn grass, and to hear the voice of Venus calling to him from the caverned hill. But at other times it speaks to me of a thousand different things, of myself, it may be, and my own life, or of the lives of others whom one has loved and grown weary of loving, or of the passions that man has known, or of the passions that man has not known, and so has sought for. To-night it may fill one with that ΕΡΩΣ ΤΩΝ ΑΔΥΝΑΤΩΝ, that 'Amour de l'Impossible,' which falls like a madness on many who think they

live securely and out of reach of harm, so that they
sicken suddenly with the poison of unlimited desire,
and, in the infinite pursuit of what they may not
obtain, grow faint and swoon or stumble.  To-
morrow, like the music of which Aristotle and Plato
tell us, the noble Dorian music of the Greek, it
may perform the office of a physician, and give us
an anodyne against pain, and heal the spirit that is
wounded, and "bring the soul into harmony with
all right things."  And what is true about music is
true about all the arts.  Beauty has as many meanings as man has moods.  Beauty is the symbol of
symbols.  Beauty reveals everything, because it
expresses nothing.  When it shows us itself, it shows
us the whole fiery-coloured world.

*Ernest.* But is such work as you have talked about
really criticism?

*Gilbert.* It is the highest Criticism, for it criticises
not merely the individual work of art, but Beauty
itself, and fills with wonder a form which the artist
may have left void, or not understood, or understood
incompletely.

*Ernest.* The highest Criticism, then, is more creative than creation, and the primary aim of the critic
is to see the object as in itself it really is not; that
is your theory, I believe?

*Gilbert.* Yes, that is my theory.  To the critic the

work of art is simply a suggestion for a new work of his own, that need not necessarily bear any obvious resemblance to the thing it criticises. The one characteristic of a beautiful form is that one can put into it whatever one wishes, and see in it whatever one chooses to see; and the Beauty, that gives to creation its universal and æsthetic element, makes the critic a creator in his turn, and whispers of a thousand different things which were not present in the mind of him who carved the statue or painted the panel or graved the gem.

It is sometimes said by those who understand neither the nature of the highest Criticism nor the charm of the highest Art, that the pictures that the critic loves most to write about are those that belong to the anecdotage of painting, and that deal with scenes taken out of literature or history. But this is not so. Indeed, pictures of this kind are far too intelligible. As a class, they rank with illustrations, and even considered from this point of view are failures, as they do not stir the imagination, but set definite bounds to it. For the domain of the painter is, as I suggested before, widely different from that of the poet. To the latter belongs life in its full and absolute entirety; not merely the beauty that men look at, but the beauty that men listen to also; not merely the momentary grace of form or the transient gladness of colour, but the whole sphere of feeling, the perfect cycle of thought. The painter is so far limited that it is only through the mask of the body that he can show us the mystery of the soul; only through conventional images that he can handle ideas; only through its physical equivalents that he can deal with psychology. And how inadequately does he do it then, asking us to accept the torn turban of the Moor for the noble rage of Othello, or a dotard in a storm for the wild madness of Lear! Yet it seems as if nothing could stop him. Most of our elderly English painters spend their wicked and wasted lives in poaching upon the domain of the poets, marring their motives by clumsy treatment, and striving to render, by visible form or colour, the marvel of what is invisible, the splendour of what is not seen. Their pictures are, as a natural consequence, insufferably tedious. They have degraded the visible arts into the obvious arts, and the one thing not worth looking at is the obvious. I do not say that poet and painter may not treat of the same subject. They have always done so, and will always do so. But while the poet can be pictorial or not, as he chooses, the painter must be pictorial always. For a painter is limited, not to what he sees in nature, but to what upon canvas may be seen.

And so, my dear Ernest, pictures of this kind will not really fascinate the critic. He will turn from them to such works as make him brood and dream and fancy, to works that possess the subtle quality of suggestion, and seem to tell one that even from them there is an escape into a wider world. It is sometimes said that the tragedy of an artist's life is that he cannot realize his ideal. But the true tragedy that dogs the steps of most artists is that they realize their ideal too absolutely. For, when the ideal is realized, it is robbed of its wonder and its mystery, and becomes simply a new starting-point for an ideal that is other than itself. This is the reason why music is the perfect type of art. Music can never reveal its ultimate secret. This, also, is the explanation of the value of limitations in art. The sculptor gladly surrenders imitative colour, and the painter the actual dimensions of form, because by such renunciations they are able to avoid too definite a presentation of the Real, which would be mere imitation, and too definite a realization of the Ideal, which would be too purely intellectual. It is through its very incompleteness that Art becomes complete in beauty, and so addresses itself, not to the faculty of recognition nor to the faculty of reason, but to the æsthetic sense alone, which, while accepting both reason and recognition as stages of apprehension, subordinates them both to a pure synthetic impression of the work of art as a whole, and, taking whatever alien emotional elements the work may possess, uses their very complexity as a means by which a richer unity may be added to the ultimate impression itself. You see, then, how it is that the æsthetic critic rejects those obvious modes of art that have but one message to deliver, and having delivered it become dumb and sterile, and seeks rather for such modes as suggest reverie and mood, and by their imaginative beauty make all interpretations true and no interpretation final.   Some resemblance, no doubt, the creative work of the critic will have to the work that has stirred him to creation, but it will be such resemblance as exists, not between Nature and the mirror that the painter of landscape or figure may be supposed to hold up to her, but between Nature and the work of the decorative artist.   Just as on the flowerless carpets of Persia, tulip and rose blossom indeed and are lovely to look on, though they are not reproduced in visible shape or line; just as the pearl and purple of the sea-shell is echoed in the church of St. Mark at Venice; just as the vaulted ceiling of the wondrous chapel of Ravenna is made gorgeous by the gold and green and sapphire of the peacock's tail, though the birds of Juno fly not across it; so the critic reproduces the work that he criticises in a mode that is never imitative, and part of whose charm may really consist in the rejection of resemblance, and shows us in this way not merely the meaning but also the mystery of Beauty, and, by transforming each art into literature, solves once for all the problem of Art's unity.

But I see it is time for supper. After we have discussed some Chambertin and a few ortolans, we will pass on to the question of the critic considered in the light of the interpreter.

*Ernest.* Ah! you admit, then, that the critic may occasionally be allowed to see the object as in itself it really is.

*Gilbert.* I am not quite sure. Perhaps, I may admit it after supper. There is a subtle influence in supper.

# THE CRITIC AS ARTIST

## WITH SOME REMARKS UPON THE IMPORTANCE OF DISCUSSING EVERYTHING

¶ *A DIALOGUE.    Part II.*
*Persons : the same.    Scene :*
*the same.*

# THE CRITIC AS ARTIST

*Ernest.* The ortolans were delightful, and the Chambertin perfect. And now let us return to the point at issue.

*Gilbert.* Ah! don't let us do that. Conversation should touch everything, but should concentrate itself on nothing. Let us talk about *Moral Indignation, its Cause and Cure*, a subject on which I think of writing: or about *The Survival of Thersites*, as shown by the English comic papers; or about any topic that may turn up.

*Ernest.* No: I want to discuss the critic and criticism. You have told me that the highest criticism deals with art, not as expressive, but as impressive purely, and is consequently both creative and independent—is, in fact, an art by itself, occupying the same relation to creative work that creative work does to the visible world of form and colour, or the unseen world of passion and of thought.

Well, now tell me, will not the critic be sometimes a real interpreter?

*Gilbert.* Yes; the critic will be an interpreter, if he chooses. He can pass from his synthetic impression of the work of art as a whole, to an analysis or exposition of the work itself, and in this lower sphere, as I hold it to be, there are many delightful things to be said and done. Yet his object will not always be to explain the work of art. He may seek rather to deepen its mystery, to raise round it, and round its maker, that mist of wonder which is dear to both gods and worshippers alike. Ordinary people are "terribly at ease in Zion." They propose to walk arm in arm with the poets, and have a glib ignorant way of saying "Why should we read what is written about Shakespeare and Milton? We can read the plays and the poems. That is enough." But an appreciation of Milton is, as the late Rector of Lincoln remarked once, the reward of consummate scholarship. And he who desires to understand Shakespeare truly must understand the relations in which Shakespeare stood to the Renaissance and the Reformation, to the age of Elizabeth and the age of James; he must be familiar with the history of the struggle for supremacy between the old classical forms and the new spirit of romance, between the school of Sidney, and

Daniel, and Jonson, and the school of Marlowe and
Marlowe's greater son; he must know the materials that were at Shakespeare's disposal, and the
method in which he used them, and the conditions
of theatric presentation in the sixteenth and seventeenth century, their limitations and their opportunities for freedom, and the literary criticism of
Shakespeare's day, its aim and modes and canons;
he must study the English language in its progress,
and blank or rhymed verse in its various developments; he must study the Greek drama, and the
connection between the art of the creator of the
Agamemnon and the art of the creator of Macbeth;
in a word, he must be able to bind Elizabethan
London to the Athens of Pericles, and to learn
Shakespeare's true position in the history of European drama and the drama of the world. The
critic will certainly be an interpreter, but he will not
treat Art as a riddling Sphinx, whose shallow secret
may be guessed and revealed by one whose feet are
wounded and who knows not his name.    Rather,
he will look upon Art as a goddess whose mystery
it is his province to intensify, and whose majesty
his privilege to make more marvellous in the eyes
of men.

And here, Ernest, this strange thing happens.
The critic will indeed be an interpreter, but he will

not be an interpreter in the sense of one who simply repeats in another form a message that has
been put into his lips to say.  For, just as it is
only by contact with the art of foreign nations that
the art of a country gains that individual and separate life that we call nationality, so, by curious
inversion, it is only by intensifying his own personality that the critic can interpret the personality
and work of others, and the more strongly this
personality enters into the interpretation the more
real the interpretation becomes, the more satisfy-
ing, the more convincing, and the more true.

*Ernest.* I would have said that personality would
have been a disturbing element.

*Gilbert.* No; it is an element of revelation.  If
you wish to understand others you must intensify
your own individualism.

*Ernest.* What, then, is the result?

*Gilbert.* I will tell you, and perhaps I can tell
you best by definite example.  It seems to me
that, while the literary critic stands of course first,
as having the wider range, and larger vision, and
nobler material, each of the arts has a critic, as it
were, assigned to it.  The actor is a critic of the
drama.  He shows the poet's work under new conditions, and by a message special to himself.  He
takes the written word, and action, gesture, and

voice become the media of revelation.   The singer,
or the player on lute and viol, is the critic of
music.   The etcher of a picture robs the painting
of its fair colours, but shows us by the use of a
new material its true colour-quality, its tones and
values, and the relations of its masses, and so is, in
his way, a critic of it, for the critic is he who ex-
hibits to us a work of art in a form different from
that of the work itself, and the employment of a
new material is a critical as well as a creative element.   Sculpture, too, has its critic, who may be
either the carver of a gem, as he was in Greek
days, or some painter like Mantegna, who sought
to reproduce on canvas the beauty of plastic line
and the symphonic dignity of processional bas-
relief.   And in the case of all these creative critics
of art it is evident that personality is an absolute
essential for any real interpretation.   When Rubin-
stein plays to us the *Sonata Appassionata* of Beethoven, he gives us not merely Beethoven, but
also himself, and so  gives us Beethoven absolutely
—Beethoven reinterpreted through a rich artistic
nature, and made vivid and wonderful to us by a
new and intense personality.   When a great actor
plays Shakespeare we have the same experience.
His own individuality becomes a vital part of
the interpretation.   People   sometimes   say   that

actors give us their own Hamlets and not Shakespeare's; and this fallacy—for it is a fallacy—is, I
regret to say, repeated by that charming and graceful writer who has lately deserted the turmoil of
literature for the peace of the House of Commons—
I mean the author of *Obiter Dicta*. In point of
fact, there is no such thing as Shakespeare's Hamlet. · If Hamlet has something of the definiteness
of a work of art, he has also all the obscurity that
belongs to life. There are as many Hamlets as
there are melancholies.

*Ernest.* As many Hamlets as there are melancholies ?

*Gilbert.* Yes : and as art springs from personality,
so it is only to personality that it can be revealed,
and from the meeting of the two comes right inter-
pretative criticism.

*Ernest.* The critic, then, considered as the interpreter, will give no less than he receives, and lend as
much as he borrows ?

*Gilbert.* He will be always showing us the work
of art in some new relation to our age. He will always be reminding us that great works of art are
living things—are, in fact, the only things that live.
So much, indeed, will he feel this, that I am certain
that, as civilization progresses and we become more
highly organized, the elect spirits of each age, the

critical and cultured spirits, will grow less and less interested in actual life, and will seek to gain their impressions almost entirely from what Art has touched. For Life is terribly deficient in form. Its catastrophes happen in the wrong way and to the wrong people. There is a grotesque horror about its comedies, and its tragedies seem to culminate in farce. One is always wounded when one approaches it. Things last either too long, or not long enough.

*Ernest.* Poor life! Poor human life! Are you not even touched by the tears that the Roman poet tells us are part of its essence?

*Gilbert.* Too quickly touched by them, I fear. For when one looks back upon the life that was so vivid in its emotional intensity, and filled with such fervent moments of ecstasy or of joy, it all seems to be a dream and an illusion. What are the unreal things, but the passions that once burned one like fire? What are the incredible things, but the things that one has faithfully believed? What are the improbable things? The things that one has done oneself. No, Ernest; life cheats us with shadows, like a puppet-master. We ask it for pleasure. It gives it to us, with bitterness and disappointment in its train. We come across some noble grief that we think will lend the purple dignity of tragedy to our days, but it passes away from us, and things less

noble take its place, and on some grey windy
dawn, or odorous eve of silence and of silver, we
find ourselves looking with callous wonder, or dull
heart of stone, at the tress of gold-flecked hair that
we had once so wildly worshipped and so madly
kissed.

*Ernest.* Life, then, is a failure?

*Gilbert.* From the artistic point of view, certainly.
And the chief thing that makes life a failure from this
artistic point of view is the thing that lends to life its
sordid security, the fact that one can never repeat
exactly the same emotion.   How different it is in the
world of Art!   On a shelf of the bookcase behind
you stands the *Divine Comedy*, and I know that, if I
open it at a certain place, I shall be filled with a
fierce hatred of some one who has never wronged me,
or stirred by a great love for some one whom I shall
never see.   There is no mood or passion that Art
cannot give us, and those of us who have discovered
her secret can settle beforehand what our experiences
are going to be.   We can choose our day and select
our hour.   We can say to ourselves, " To-morrow,
at dawn, we shall walk with grave Virgil through
the valley of the shadow of death," and lo! the
dawn finds us in the obscure wood, and the Mantuan
stands by our side.   We pass through the gate of the
legend fatal to hope, and with pity or with joy be-

hold the horror of another world. The hypocrites go by, with their painted faces and their cowls of gilded lead. Out of the ceaseless winds that drive them, the carnal look at us, and we watch the heretic rending his flesh, and the glutton lashed by the rain. We break the withered branches from the tree in the grove of the Harpies, and each dull-hued poisonous twig bleeds with red blood before us, and cries aloud with bitter cries. Out of a horn of fire Odysseus speaks to us, and when from his sepulchre of flame the great Ghibelline rises, the pride that triumphs over the torture of that bed becomes ours for a moment. Through the dim purple air fly those who have stained the world with the beauty of their sin, and in the pit of loathsome disease, dropsy-stricken and swollen of body into the semblance of a monstrous lute, lies Adamo di Brescia, the coiner of false coin. He bids us listen to his misery; we stop, and with dry and gaping lips he tells us how he dreams day and night of the brooks of clear water that in cool dewy channels gush down the green Casentine hills. Sinon, the false Greek of Troy, mocks at him. He smites him in the face, and they wrangle. We are fascinated by their shame, and loiter, till Virgil chides us and leads us away to that city turreted by giants where great Nimrod blows his horn. Terrible things are in store for us, and we go to meet them in Dante's raiment and with Dante's heart. We traverse the marshes of the Styx, and Argenti swims to the boat through the slimy waves. He calls to us, and we reject him. When we hear the voice of his agony we are glad, and Virgil praises us for the bitterness of our scorn. We tread upon the cold crystal of Cocytus, in which traitors stick like straws in glass. Our foot strikes against the head of Bocca. He will not tell us his name, and we tear the hair in handfuls from the screaming skull. Alberigo prays us to break the ice upon his face that he may weep a little. We pledge our word to him, and when he has uttered his dolorous tale we deny the word that we have spoken, and pass from him; such cruelty being courtesy indeed, for who more base than he who has mercy for the condemned of God? In the jaws of Lucifer we see the man who sold Christ, and in the jaws of Lucifer the men who slew Cæsar. We tremble, and come forth to rebehold the stars.

In the land of Purgation the air is freer, and the holy mountain rises into the pure light of day. There is peace for us, and for those who for a season abide in it there is some peace also, though, pale from the poison of the Maremma, Madonna Pia passes before us, and Ismene, with the sorrow of earth still lingering about her, is there. Soul after soul makes us

share in some repentance or some joy. He whom
the mourning of his widow taught to drink the sweet
wormwood of pain, tells us of Nella praying in her
lonely bed, and we learn from the mouth of Buon-
conte how a single tear may save a dying sinner from
the fiend. Sordello, that noble and disdainful Lom-
bard, eyes us from afar like a couchant lion. When
he learns that Virgil is one of Mantua's citizens, he
falls upon his neck, and when he learns that he is the
singer of Rome he falls before his feet. In that valley whose grass and flowers are fairer than cleft
emerald and Indian wood, and brighter than scarlet
and silver, they are singing who in the world were
kings; but the lips of Rudolph of Hapsburg do not
move to the music of the others, and Philip of France
beats his breast and Henry of England sits alone.
On and on we go, climbing the marvellous stair, and
the stars become larger than their wont, and the song
of the kings grows faint, and at length we reach the
seven trees of gold and the garden of the Earthly
Paradise. In a griffin-drawn chariot appears one
whose brows are bound with olive, who is veiled in
white, and mantled in green, and robed in a vesture
that is coloured like live fire. The ancient flame
wakes within us. Our blood quickens through terrible pulses. We recognize her. It is Beatrice, the woman we have worshipped. The ice congealed about

our heart melts.  Wild tears of anguish break from us, and we bow our forehead to the ground, for we know that we have sinned.  When we have done penance, and are purified, and have drunk of the fountain of Lethe and bathed in the fountain of Eunoe, the mistress of our soul raises us to the Paradise of Heaven.  Out of that eternal pearl, the moon, the face of Piccarda Donati leans to us.  Her beauty troubles us for a moment, and when, like a thing that falls through water, she passes away, we gaze after her with wistful eyes.  The sweet planet of Venus is full of lovers.  Cunizza, the sister of Ezzelin, the lady of Sordello's heart, is there, and Folco, the passionate singer of Provence, who in sorrow for Azalais forsook the world, and the Canaanitish harlot whose soul was the first that Christ redeemed.  Joachim of Flora stands in the sun, and, in the sun, Aquinas recounts the story of St. Francis and Bonaventure the story of St. Dominic.  Through the burning rubies of Mars, Cacciaguida approaches.  He tells us of the arrow that is shot from the bow of exile, and how salt tastes the bread of another, and how steep are the stairs in the house of a stranger.  In Saturn the souls sing not, and even she who guides us dare not smile.  On a ladder of gold the flames rise and fall.  At last, we see the pageant of the Mystical Rose.  Beatrice fixes her eyes upon the face of God, to turn them not again. The beatific vision is granted to us; we know the Love that moves the sun and all the stars.

Yes, we can put the earth back six hundred courses and make ourselves one with the great Florentine, kneel at the same altar with him, and share his rapture and his scorn. And if we grow tired of an antique time, and desire to realize our own age in all its weariness and sin, are there not books that can make us live more in one single hour than life can make us live in a score of shameful years? Close to your hand lies a little volume, bound in some Nile-green skin that has been powdered with gilded nenuphars and smoothed with hard ivory. It is the book that Gautier loved, it is Baudelaire's masterpiece. Open it at that sad madrigal that begins

> " Que m'importe que tu sois sage?
> Sois belle ! et sois triste ! "

and you will find yourself worshipping sorrow as you have never worshipped joy. Pass on to the poem on the man who tortures himself, let its subtle music steal into your brain and colour your thoughts, and you will become for a moment what he was who wrote it; nay, not for a moment only, but for many barren moonlit nights and sunless sterile days will a despair that is not your own make its dwelling within

you, and the misery of another gnaw your heart
away. Read the whole book, suffer it to tell even one
of its secrets to your soul, and your soul will grow
eager to know more, and will feed upon poisonous
honey, and seek to repent of strange crimes of which
it is guiltless, and to make atonement for terrible
pleasures that it has never known. And then, when
you are tired of these flowers of evil, turn to the
flowers that grow in the garden of Perdita, and in
their dew-drenched chalices cool your fevered brow,
and let their loveliness heal and restore your soul;
or wake from his forgotten tomb the sweet Syrian,
Meleager, and bid the lover of Heliodore make you
music, for he too has flowers in his song, red pome-
granate-blossoms, and irises that smell of myrrh,
ringed daffodils and dark-blue hyacinths, and mar-
joram and crinkled ox-eyes. Dear to him was the
perfume of the bean-field at evening, and dear to him
the odorous eared-spikenard that grew on the Syrian
hills, and the fresh green thyme, the wine-cup's
charm. The feet of his love as she walked in the
garden were like lilies set upon lilies. Softer than
sleep-laden poppy-petals were her lips, softer than
violets and as scented. The flame-like crocus sprang
from the grass to look at her. For her the slim
narcissus stored the cool rain; and for her the
anemones forgot the Sicilian winds that wooed

them. And neither crocus, nor anemone, nor narcissus was as fair as she was.

It is a strange thing, this transference of emotion. We sicken with the same maladies as the poets, and the singer lends us his pain. Dead lips have their message for us, and hearts that have fallen to dust can communicate their joy. We run to kiss the bleeding mouth of Fantine, and we follow Manon Lescaut over the whole world. Ours is the love-madness of the Tyrian, and the terror of Orestes is ours also. There is no passion that we cannot feel, no pleasure that we may not gratify, and we can choose the time of our initiation and the time of our freedom also. Life! Life! Don't let us go to life for our fulfilment or our experience. It is a thing narrowed by circumstances, incoherent in its utterance, and without that fine correspondence of form and spirit which is the only thing that can satisfy the artistic and critical temperament. It makes us pay too high a price for its wares, and we purchase the meanest of its secrets at a cost that is monstrous and infinite.

*Ernest.* Must we go, then, to Art for everything?

*Gilbert.* For everything. Because Art does not hurt us. The tears that we shed at a play are a type of the exquisite sterile emotions that it is the function of Art to awaken. We weep, but we are

not wounded.   We grieve, but our grief is not bitter.
In the actual life of man, sorrow, as Spinoza says
somewhere, is a passage to a lesser perfection.   But
the sorrow with which Art fills us both purifies and
initiates, if I may quote once more from the great
art-critic of the Greeks.   It is through Art, and
through Art only, that we can realize our perfection; through Art, and through Art only, that we
can shield ourselves from the sordid perils of actual
existence.   This results not merely from the fact
that nothing that one can imagine is worth doing,
and that one can imagine everything, but from the
subtle law that emotional forces, like the forces of
the physical sphere, are limited in extent and energy.
One can feel so much, and no more.   And how can
it matter with what pleasure life tries to tempt one,
or with what pain it seeks to maim and mar one's
soul, if in the spectacle of the lives of those who have
never existed one has found the true secret of joy,
and wept away one's tears over their deaths who,
like Cordelia and the daughter of Brabantio, can
never die?

*Ernest.* Stop a moment.   It seems to me that in
everything that you have said there is something
radically immoral.

*Gilbert.* All art is immoral.

*Ernest.* All art?

*Gilbert.* Yes. For emotion for the sake of emotion is the aim of art, and emotion for the sake of action is the aim of life, and of that practical organization of life that we call society. Society, which is the beginning and basis of morals, exists simply for the concentration of human energy, and in order to ensure its own continuance and healthy stability it demands, and no doubt rightly demands, of each of its citizens that he should contribute some form of productive labor to the common weal, and toil and travail that the day's work may be done. Society often forgives the criminal; it never forgives the dreamer. The beautiful sterile emotions that art excites in us, are hateful in its eyes, and so completely are people dominated by the tyranny of this dreadful social ideal that they are always coming shamelessly up to one at Private Views and other places that are open to the general public, and saying in a loud stentorian voice, "What are you doing?" whereas "What are you thinking?" is the only question that any single civilized being should ever be allowed to whisper to another. They mean well, no doubt, these honest beaming folk. Perhaps that is the reason why they are so excessively tedious. But some one should teach them that while, in the opinion of society, Contemplation is the gravest sin of which any citizen can be guilty, in the opinion of the highest culture it is the proper occupation of man.

*Ernest.* Contemplation?

*Gilbert.* Contemplation. I said to you some time ago that it was far more difficult to talk about a thing than to do it. Let me say to you now that to do nothing at all is the most difficult thing in the world, the most difficult and the most intellectual. To Plato, with his passion for wisdom, this was the noblest form of energy. To Aristotle, with his passion for knowledge, this was the noblest form of energy also. It was to this that the passion for holiness led the saint and the mystic of mediæval days.

*Ernest.* We exist, then, to do nothing?

*Gilbert.* It is to do nothing that the elect exist. Action is limited and relative. Unlimited and absolute is the vision of him who sits at ease and watches, who walks in loneliness and dreams. But we who are born at the close of this wonderful age, are at once too cultured and too critical, too intellectually subtle and too curious of exquisite pleasures, to accept any speculations about life in exchange for life itself. To us the 'citta divina' is colourless, and the 'fruitio Dei' without meaning. Metaphysics do not satisfy our temperaments, and religious ecstasy is out of date. The world through

which the Academic philosopher becomes "the
spectator of all time and of all existence" is not
really an ideal world, but simply a world of abstract
ideas. When we enter it, we starve amidst the chill
mathematics of thought. The courts of the city of
God are not open to us now. Its gates are guarded
by Ignorance, and to pass them we have to surrender all that in our nature is most divine. It is
enough that our fathers believed. They have exhausted the faith-faculty of the species. Their
legacy to us is the scepticism of which they were
afraid. Had they put it into words, it might not
live within us as thought. No, Ernest, no. We
cannot go back to the saint. There is far more to
be learned from the sinner. We cannot go back to
the philosopher, and the mystic leads us astray.
Who, as Mr. Pater suggests somewhere, would exchange the curve of a single rose-leaf for that form-
less intangible Being which Plato rates so high?
What to us is the Illumination of Philo, the Abyss
of Eckhart, the Vision of Böhme, the monstrous
Heaven itself that was revealed to Swedenborg's
blinded eyes? Such things are less than the yellow
trumpet of one daffodil of the field, far less than the
meanest of the visible arts; for, just as Nature is
matter struggling into mind, so Art is mind expressing itself under the conditions of matter, and

thus, even in the lowliest of her manifestations, she speaks to both sense and soul alike. To the æsthetic temperament the vague is always repellent. The Greeks were a nation of artists, because they were spared the sense of the infinite. Like Aristotle, like Goethe after he had read Kant, we desire the concrete, and nothing but the concrete can satisfy us.

*Ernest.* What then do you propose?

*Gilbert.* It seems to me that with the development of the critical spirit we shall be able to realize, not merely our own lives, but the collective life of the race, and so to make ourselves absolutely modern, in the true meaning of the word modernity. For he to whom the present is the only thing that is present, knows nothing of the age in which he lives. To realize the nineteenth century, one must realize every century that has preceded it and that has contributed to its making. To know anything about oneself, one must know all about others. There must be no mood with which one cannot sympathize, no dead mode of life that one cannot make alive. Is this impossible? I think not. By revealing to us the absolute mechanism of all action, and so freeing us from the self-imposed and trammelling burden of moral responsibility, the scientific principle of Heredity has become, as it were, the warrant for the contemplative life. It has shown us that we are never less free than when we try to act. It has hemmed us round with the nets of the hunter, and written upon the wall the prophecy of our doom. We may not watch it, for it is within us. We may not see it, save in a mirror that mirrors the soul. It is Nemesis without her mask. It is the last of the Fates, and the most terrible. It is the only one of the Gods whose real name we know.

And yet, while in the sphere of practical and external life it has robbed energy of its freedom and activity of its choice, in the subjective sphere, where the soul is at work, it comes to us, this terrible shadow, with many gifts in its hands, gifts of strange temperaments and subtle susceptibilities, gifts of wild ardours and chill moods of indifference, complex multiform gifts of thoughts that are at variance with each other, and passions that war against themselves. And so, it is not our own life that we live, but the lives of the dead, and the soul that dwells within us is no single spiritual entity, making us personal and individual, created for our service, and entering into us for our joy. It is something that has dwelt in fearful places, and in ancient sepulchres has made its abode. It is sick with many maladies, and has memories of curious

sins.  It is wiser than we are, and its wisdom is
bitter.  It fills us with impossible desires, and
makes us follow what we know we cannot gain.
One thing, however, Ernest, it can do for us.
It can lead us away from surroundings whose
beauty is dimmed to us by the mist of familiar-
ity, or whose ignoble ugliness and sordid claims
are marring the perfection of our development.  It
can help us to leave the age in which we were born,
and to pass into other ages, and find ourselves not
exiled from their air.  It can teach us how to escape
from our experience, and to realize the experiences
of those who are greater than we are.  The pain of
Leopardi crying out against life becomes our pain.
Theocritus blows on his pipe, and we laugh with
the lips of nymph and shepherd.  In the wolfskin
of Pierre Vidal we flee before the hounds, and in
the armour of Lancelot we ride from the bower of
the Queen.  We have whispered the secret of our
love beneath the cowl of Abelard, and in the stained
raiment of Villon have put our shame into song.
We can see the dawn through Shelley's eyes, and
when we wander with Endymion the Moon grows
amorous of our youth.  Ours is the anguish of
Atys, and ours the weak rage and noble sorrows of
the Dane.  Do you think that it is the imagination
that enables us to live these countless lives?  Yes:

it is the imagination; and the imagination is the result of heredity.  It is simply concentrated race-experience.

*Ernest.* But where in this is the function of the critical spirit?

*Gilbert.* The culture that this transmission of racial experiences makes possible can be made perfect by the critical spirit alone, and indeed may be said to be one with it.  For who is the true critic but he who bears within himself the dreams, and ideas, and feelings of myriad generations, and to whom no form of thought is alien, no emotional impulse obscure?  And who the true man of culture, if not he who by fine scholarship and fastidious rejection has made instinct self-conscious and intelligent, and can separate the work that has distinction from the work that has it not, and so by contact and comparison makes himself master of the secrets of style and school, and understands their meanings, and listens to their voices, and develops that spirit of disinterested curiosity which is the real root, as it is the real flower, of the intellectual life, and thus attains to intellectual clarity, and, having learned " the best that is known and thought in the world," lives—it is not fanciful to say so—with those who are the Immortals.

Yes, Ernest: the contemplative life, the life that

has for its aim not *doing* but *being*, and not *being*
merely, but *becoming*—that is what the critical
spirit can give us.  The gods live thus: either
brooding over their own perfection, as Aristotle
tells us, or, as Epicurus fancied, watching with
the calm eyes of the spectator the tragi-comedy of
the world that they have made.  We, too, might
live like them, and set ourselves to witness with
appropriate emotions the varied scenes that man
and nature afford.  We might make ourselves
spiritual by detaching ourselves from action, and
become perfect by the rejection of energy.  It has
often seemed to me that Browning felt something
of this.  Shakespeare hurls Hamlet into active
life, and makes him realize his mission by effort.
Browning might have given us a Hamlet who
would have realized his mission by thought.  Incident and event were to him unreal or unmeaning.
He made the soul the protagonist of life's tragedy,
and looked on action as the one undramatic element of a play.  To us, at any rate, the ΒΙΟΣ
ΘΕΩΡΗΤΙΚΟΣ is the true ideal.  From the high
tower of Thought we can look out at the world.
Calm, and self-centred, and complete, the æsthetic
critic contemplates life, and no arrow drawn at a
venture can pierce between the joints of his harness.
He at least is safe.  He has discovered how to
live.

Is such a mode of life immoral? Yes: all the
arts are immoral, except those baser forms of sensual or didactic art that seek to excite to action of
evil or of good.    For action of every kind belongs
to the sphere of ethics.    The aim of art is simply to
create a mood.    Is such a mode of life unpractical?
Ah! it is not so easy to be unpractical as the
ignorant Philistine imagines.    It were well for England if it were so.    There is no country in the
world so much in need of unpractical people as
this country of ours.    With us, Thought is degraded by its constant association with practice.
Who that moves in the stress and turmoil of actual
existence, noisy politician, or brawling social re-
former, or poor narrow-minded priest blinded by
the sufferings of that unimportant section of the
community among whom he has cast his lot, can
seriously claim to be able to form a disinterested
intellectual judgment about any one thing?    Each
of the professions means a prejudice.    The necessity for a career forces every one to take sides.
We live in the age of the overworked, and the
under-educated; the age in which people are so
industrious that they become absolutely stupid.
And, harsh though it may sound, I cannot help saying that such people deserve their doom.    The
sure way of knowing nothing about life is to try to
make oneself useful.

*Ernest.* A charming doctrine, Gilbert.

*Gilbert.* I am not sure about that, but it has at least the minor merit of being true. That the desire to do good to others produces a plentiful crop of prigs is the least of the evils of which it is the cause. The prig is a very interesting psychological study, and though of all poses a moral pose is the most offensive, still to have a pose at all is something. It is a formal recognition of the importance of treating life from a definite and reasoned standpoint. That Humanitarian Sympathy wars against Nature, by securing the survival of the failure, may make the man of science loathe its facile virtues. The political economist may cry out against it for putting the improvident on the same level as the provident, and so robbing life of the strongest, because most sordid, incentive to industry. But, in the eyes of the thinker, the real harm that emotional sympathy does is that it limits knowledge, and so prevents us from solving any single social problem. We are trying at present to stave off the coming crisis, the coming revolution, as my friends, the Fabianists, call it, by means of doles and alms. Well, when the revolution or crisis arrives we shall be powerless because we shall know nothing. And so, Ernest, let us not be deceived. England will never be civilized till she has added Utopia to her

dominions.   There is more than one of her colonies
that she might with advantage surrender for so fair
a land.   What we want are unpractical people who
see beyond the moment, and think beyond the day.
Those who try to lead the people can only do so
by following the mob.   It is through the voice of
one crying in the wilderness that the ways of the
gods must be prepared.

But perhaps you think that in beholding for the
mere joy of beholding, and contemplating for the
sake of contemplation, there is something that is
egotistic.   If you think so, do not say so.   It takes
a thoroughly selfish age, like our own, to deify self-
sacrifice.   It takes a thoroughly grasping age, such
as that in which we live, to set above the fine intellectual virtues, those shallow and emotional virtues
that are an immediate practical benefit to itself.  They
miss their aim, too, these philanthropists and sentimentalists of our day, who are always chattering to
one about one's duty to one's neighbour.   For the
development of the race depends on the development of the individual, and where self-culture has
ceased to be the ideal, the intellectual standard is
instantly lowered, and, often, ultimately lost.   If
you meet at dinner a man who has spent his life in
educating himself—a rare type in our time, I
admit, but still one occasionally to be met with—

you rise from table richer, and conscious that a
high ideal has for a moment touched and sanctified
your days.    But, oh! my dear Ernest, to sit next
a man who has spent his life in trying to educate
others!    What a dreadful experience that is!
How appalling is that ignorance which is the inevitable result of the fatal habit of imparting opinions!    How limited in range the creature's mind
proves to be!    How it wearies us, and must weary
himself, with its endless repetitions and sickly reiteration!    How lacking it is in any element of
intellectual growth!    In what a vicious circle it
always moves!

*Ernest.*    You speak with strange feeling, Gilbert.
Have you had this dreadful experience, as you call
it, lately?

*Gilbert.*    Few of us escape it.    People say that
the schoolmaster is abroad.    I wish to goodness
he were.    But the type of which, after all, he is
only one, and certainly the least important, of the
representatives, seems to me to be really domi-
nating our lives; and just as the philanthropist is
the nuisance of the ethical sphere, so the nuisance
of the intellectual sphere is the man who is so occupied in trying to educate others, that he has never
had any time to educate himself.    No, Ernest,
self-culture is the true ideal of man.    Goethe saw

it, and the immediate debt that we owe to Goethe is greater than the debt we owe to any man since Greek days. The Greeks saw it, and have left us, as their legacy to modern thought, the conception of the contemplative life as well as the critical method by which alone can that life be truly realized. It was the one thing that made the Renaissance great, and gave us Humanism. It is the one thing that could make our own age great also; for the real weakness of England lies, not in incomplete armaments or unfortified coasts, not in the poverty that creeps through sunless lanes, or the drunkenness that brawls in loathsome courts, but simply in the fact that her ideals are emotional and not intellectual.

I do not deny that the intellectual ideal is difficult of attainment, still less that it is, and perhaps will be for years to come, unpopular with the crowd. It is so easy for people to have sympathy with suffering. It is so difficult for them to have sympathy with thought. Indeed, so little do ordinary people understand what thought really is, that they seem to imagine that, when they have said that a theory is dangerous, they have pronounced its condemnation, whereas it is only such theories that have any true intellectual value. An idea that is not dangerous is unworthy of being called an idea at all.

*Ernest.* Gilbert, you bewilder me.   You have told me that all art is, in its essence, immoral.   Are you going to tell me now that all thought is, in its essence, dangerous?

*Gilbert.* Yes, in the practical sphere it is so.   The security of society lies in custom and unconscious instinct, and the basis of the stability of society, as a healthy organism, is the complete absence of any intelligence amongst its members.   The great majority of people, being fully aware of this, rank themselves naturally on the side of that splendid system that elevates them to the dignity of machines, and rage so wildly against the intrusion of the intellectual faculty into any question that concerns life, that one is tempted to define man as a rational animal who always loses his temper when he is called upon to act in accordance with the dictates of reason.   But let us turn from the practical sphere, and say no more about the wicked philanthropists, who, indeed, may well be left to the mercy of the almond-eyed sage of the Yellow River, Chuang Tsŭ the wise, who has proved that such well-meaning and offensive busybodies have destroyed the simple and spontaneous virtue that there is in man.   They are a wearisome topic, and I am anxious to get back to the sphere in which criticism is free.

*Ernest.* The sphere of the intellect?

*Gilbert.* Yes. You remember that I spoke of the critic as being in his own way as creative as the artist, whose work, indeed, may be merely of value in so far as it gives to the critic a suggestion for some new mood of thought and feeling which he can realize with equal, or perhaps greater, distinction of form, and, through the use of a fresh medium of expression, make differently beautiful and more perfect. Well, you seemed to me to be a little sceptical about the theory. But perhaps I wronged you?

*Ernest.* I am not really sceptical about it, but I must admit that I feel very strongly that such work as you describe the critic producing—and creative such work must undoubtedly be admitted to be—is, of necessity, purely subjective, whereas the greatest work is objective always, objective and impersonal.

*Gilbert.* The difference between objective and subjective work is one of external form merely. It is accidental, not essential. All artistic creation is absolutely subjective. The very landscape that Corot looked at was, as he said himself, but a mood of his own mind; and those great figures of Greek or English drama that seem to us to possess an actual existence of their own, apart from the poets who shaped and fashioned them, are, in their ultimate analysis, simply the poets themselves, not as they thought they were, but as they thought they were not; and

by such thinking came in strange manner, though
but for a moment, really so to be.   For out of ourselves we can never pass, nor can there be in creation
what in the creator was not.   Nay, I would say that
the more objective a creation appears to be, the more
subjective it really is.   Shakespeare might have met
Rosencrantz and Guildenstern in the white streets of
London, or seen the serving-men of rival houses bite
their thumbs at each other in the open square; but
Hamlet came out of his soul, and Romeo out of his
passion.   They were elements of his nature to which
he gave visible form, impulses that stirred so strongly
within him that he had, as it were perforce, to suffer
them to realize their energy, not on the lower plane
of actual life, where they would have been tram-
melled and constrained and so made imperfect, but on
that imaginative plane of art where Love can indeed
find in Death its rich fulfilment, where one can stab
the eavesdropper behind the arras, and wrestle in a
new-made grave, and make a guilty king drink his
own hurt, and see one's father's spirit, beneath the
glimpses of the moon, stalking in complete steel
from misty wall to wall.   Action being limited would
have left Shakespeare unsatisfied and unexpressed;
and, just as it is because he did nothing that he has
been able to achieve everything, so it is because he
never speaks to us of himself in his plays that his

plays reveal him to us absolutely, and show us his true nature and temperament far more completely than do those strange and exquisite sonnets, even, in which he bares to crystal eyes the secret closet of his heart. Yes, the objective form is the most subjective in matter. Man is least himself when he talks in his own person. Give him a mask, and he will tell you the truth.

*Ernest.* The critic, then, being limited to the subjective form, will necessarily be less able to fully express himself than the artist, who has always at his disposal the forms that are impersonal and objective.

*Gilbert.* Not necessarily, and certainly not at all if he recognizes that each mode of criticism is, in its highest development, simply a mood, and that we are never more true to ourselves than when we are inconsistent. The æsthetic critic, constant only to the principle of beauty in all things, will ever be looking for fresh impressions, winning from the various schools the secret of their charm, bowing, it may be, before foreign altars, or smiling, if it be his fancy, at strange new gods. What other people call one's past has, no doubt, everything to do with them, but has absolutely nothing to do with oneself. The man who regards his past is a man who deserves to have no future to look forward to. When one has found expression for a mood, one has done with it. You

laugh; but believe me it is so.   Yesterday it was
Realism that charmed one.   One gained from it that
‘nouveau frisson’ which it was its aim to produce.
One analysed it, explained it, and wearied of it.   At
sunset came the ‘Luministe’ in painting, and the
‘Symboliste’ in poetry, and the spirit of mediævalism, that spirit which belongs not to time but to
temperament, woke suddenly in wounded Russia,
and stirred us for a moment by the terrible fascination of pain.   To-day the cry is for Romance, and
already the leaves are tremulous in the valley, and on
the purple hill-tops walks Beauty with slim gilded
feet.   The old modes of creation linger, of course.
The artists reproduce either themselves or each
other, with wearisome iteration.   But Criticism is
always moving on, and the critic is always develop-
ing.

Nor, again, is the critic really limited to the subjective form of expression.   The method of the drama
is his, as well as the method of the epos.   He may
use dialogue, as he did who set Milton talking to
Marvel on the nature of comedy and tragedy, and
made Sidney and Lord Brooke discourse on letters
beneath the Penshurst oaks; or adopt narration, as
Mr. Pater is fond of doing, each of whose Imaginary
Portraits—is not that the title of the book?—presents to us, under the fanciful guise of fiction, some

fine and exquisite piece of criticism, one on the painter Watteau, another on the philosophy of Spinoza, a third on the Pagan elements of the early Renaissance, and the last, and in some respects the most suggestive, on the source of that Aufklärung, that enlightening which dawned on Germany in the last century, and to which our own culture owes so great a debt. Dialogue, certainly, that wonderful literary form which, from Plato to Lucian, and from Lucian to Giordano Bruno, and from Bruno to that grand old Pagan in whom Carlyle took such delight, the creative critics of the world have always employed, can never lose for the thinker its attraction as a mode of expression. By its means he can both reveal and conceal himself, and give form to every fancy, and reality to every mood. By its means he can exhibit the object from each point of view, and show it to us in the round, as a sculptor shows us things, gaining in this manner all the richness and reality of effect that comes from those side issues that are suddenly suggested by the central idea in its progress, and really illumine the idea more completely, or from those felicitous after-thoughts that give a fuller completeness to the central scheme, and yet convey something of the delicate charm of chance.

*Ernest.* By its means, too, he can invent an

imaginary antagonist, and convert him when he chooses by some absurdly sophistical argument.

*Gilbert.* Ah! it is so easy to convert others. It is so difficult to convert oneself. To arrive at what one really believes, one must speak through lips different from one's own. To know the truth one must imagine myriads of falsehoods. For what is Truth? In matters of religion, it is simply the opinion that has survived. In matters of science, it is the ultimate sensation. In matters of art, it is one's last mood. And you see now, Ernest, that the critic has at his disposal as many objective forms of expression as the artist has. Ruskin put his criticism into imaginative prose, and is superb in his changes and contradictions; and Browning put his into blank verse, and made painter and poet yield us their secret; and M. Renan uses dialogue, and Mr. Pater fiction, and Rossetti translated into sonnet-music the colour of Giorgione and the design of Ingres, and his own design and colour also, feeling, with the instinct of one who had many modes of utterance, that the ultimate art is literature, and the finest and fullest medium that of words.

*Ernest.* Well, now that you have settled that the critic has at his disposal all objective forms, I wish you would tell me what are the qualities that should characterize the true critic.

*Gilbert.* What would you say they were?

*Ernest.* Well, I should say that a critic should above all things be fair.

*Gilbert.* Ah! not fair. A critic cannot be fair in the ordinary sense of the word. It is only about things that do not interest one that one can give a really unbiassed opinion, which is no doubt the reason why an unbiassed opinion is always absolutely valueless. The man who sees both sides of a question, is a man who sees absolutely nothing at all. Art is a passion, and, in matters of art, Thought is inevitably coloured by emotion, and so is fluid rather than fixed, and, depending upon fine moods and exquisite moments, cannot be narrowed into the rigidity of a scientific formula or a theological dogma. It is to the soul that Art speaks, and the soul may be made the prisoner of the mind as well as of the body. One should, of course, have no prejudices; but, as a great Frenchman remarked a hundred years ago, it is one's business in such matters to have preferences, and when one has preferences one ceases to be fair. It is only an auctioneer who can equally and impartially admire all schools of Art. No: fairness is not one of the qualities of the true critic. It is not even a condition of criticism. Each form of Art with which we come in contact dominates us for the moment to the exclusion of every other form. We must surrender ourselves absolutely to the work in question, whatever it may be, if we wish to gain its secret. For the time, we must think of nothing else, can think of nothing else, indeed.

*Ernest.* The true critic will be rational, at any rate, will he not?

*Gilbert.* Rational? There are two ways of disliking art, Ernest. One is to dislike it. The other, to like it rationally. For Art, as Plato saw, and not without regret, creates in listener and spectator a form of divine madness. It does not spring from inspiration, but it makes others inspired. Reason is not the faculty to which it appeals. If one loves Art at all, one must love it beyond all other things in the world, and against such love, the reason, if one listened to it, would cry out. There is nothing sane about the worship of beauty. It is too splendid to be sane. Those of whose lives it forms the dominant note will always seem to the world to be pure visionaries.

*Ernest.* Well, at least, the critic will be sincere.

*Gilbert.* A little sincerity is a dangerous thing, and a great deal of it is absolutely fatal. The true critic will, indeed, always be sincere in his devotion to the principle of beauty, but he will seek for beauty in every age and in each school, and will

never suffer himself to be limited to any settled
custom of thought, or stereotyped mode of looking
at things.   He will realize himself in many forms,
and by a thousand different ways, and will ever be
curious of new sensations and fresh points of view.
Through constant change, and through constant
change alone, he will find his true unity.   He will
not consent to be the slave of his own opinions.
For what is mind but motion in the intellectual
sphere?   The essence of thought, as the essence of
life, is growth.   You must not be frightened by
words, Ernest.   What people call insincerity is
simply a method by which we can multiply our
personalities.

*Ernest.* I am afraid I have not been fortunate in
my suggestions.

*Gilbert.* Of the three qualifications you mentioned, two, sincerity and fairness, were, if not
actually moral, at least on the border-land of morals,
and the first condition of criticism is that the critic
should be able to recognize that the sphere of Art
and the sphere of Ethics are absolutely distinct and
separate.   When they are confused, Chaos has
come again.   They are too often confused in England now, and though our modern Puritans cannot
destroy a beautiful thing, yet, by means of their
extraordinary prurience, they can almost taint

beauty for a moment. It is chiefly, I regret to
say, through journalism that such people find expression. I regret it because there is much to be
said in favor of modern journalism. By giving us
the opinions of the uneducated, it keeps us in touch
with the ignorance of the community. By carefully
chronicling the current events of contemporary
life, it shows us of what very little importance such
events really are. By invariably discussing the unnecessary, it makes us understand what things are
requisite for culture, and what are not. But it
should not allow poor Tartuffe to write articles
upon modern art. When it does this it stultifies
itself. And yet Tartuffe's articles, and Chadband's
notes, do this good, at least. They serve to show
how extremely limited is the area over which
ethics, and ethical considerations, can claim to
exercise influence. Science is out of the reach of
morals, for her eyes are fixed upon eternal truths.
Art is out of the reach of morals, for her eyes are
fixed upon things beautiful and immortal and ever-
changing. To morals belong the lower and less
intellectual spheres. However, let these mouthing
Puritans pass; they have their comic side. Who
can help laughing when an ordinary journalist
seriously proposes to limit the subject-matter at the
disposal of the artist? Some limitation might

well, and will soon, I hope, be placed upon some of our newspapers and newspaper writers. For they give us the bald, sordid, disgusting facts of life. They chronicle, with degrading avidity, the sins of the second-rate, and with the conscientiousness of the illiterate give us accurate and prosaic details of the doings of people of absolutely no interest whatsoever. But the artist, who accepts the facts of life, and yet transforms them into shapes of beauty, and makes them vehicles of pity or of awe, and shows their colour-element, and their wonder, and their true ethical import also, and builds out of them a world more real than reality itself, and of loftier and more noble import—who shall set limits to him? Not the apostles of that new Journalism which is but the old vulgarity "writ large." Not the apostles of that new Puritanism, which is but the whine of the hypocrite, and is both writ and spoken badly. The mere suggestion is ridiculous. Let us leave these wicked people, and proceed to the discussion of the artistic qualifications necessary for the true critic.

*Ernest.* And what are they? Tell me yourself.

*Gilbert.* Temperament is the primary requisite for the critic—a temperament exquisitely susceptible to beauty, and to the various impressions that beauty gives us. Under what conditions, and by what means, this temperament is engendered in race or individual, we will not discuss at present. It is sufficient to note that it exists, and that there is in us a beauty-sense, separate from the other senses and above them, separate from the reason and of nobler import, separate from the soul and of equal value— a sense that leads some to create, and others, the finer spirits as I think, to contemplate merely. But to be purified and made perfect, this sense requires some form of exquisite environment. Without this it starves, or is dulled. You remember that lovely passage in which Plato describes how a young Greek should be educated, and with what insistence he dwells upon the importance of surroundings, telling us how the lad is to be brought up in the midst of fair sights and sounds, so that the beauty of material things may prepare his soul for the reception of the beauty that is spiritual. Insensibly, and without knowing the reason why, he is to develop that real love of beauty which, as Plato is never weary of reminding us, is the true aim of education. By slow degrees there is to be engendered in him such a temperament as will lead him naturally and simply to choose the good in preference to the bad, and, rejecting what is vulgar and discordant, to follow by fine instinctive taste all that possesses grace and charm and loveli-

ness.  Ultimately, in its due course, this taste is to
become critical and self-conscious, but at first it
is to exist purely as a cultivated instinct, and " he
who has received this true culture of the inner man
will with clear and certain vision perceive the omis-
sions and faults in art or nature, and with a taste
that cannot err, while he praises, and finds his pleasure in what is good, and receives it into his soul, and
so becomes good and noble, he will rightly blame
and hate the bad, now in the days of his youth, even
before he is able to know the reason why : " and so,
when, later on, the critical and self-conscious spirit
develops in him, he " will recognize and salute it as
a friend with whom his education has made him long
familiar."   I need hardly say, Ernest, how far we in
England have fallen short of this ideal, and I can
imagine the smile that would illuminate the glossy
face of the Philistine if one ventured to suggest to
him that the true aim of education was the love of
beauty, and that the methods by which education
should work were the development of temperament,
the cultivation of taste, and the creation of the critical spirit.

Yet, even for us, there is left some loveliness of
environment, and the dulness of tutors and profes-
sors matters very little when one can loiter in the
grey cloisters at Magdalen, and listen to some flute-

like voice singing in Waynfleete's chapel, or lie in
the green meadow, among the strange snake-spotted
fritillaries, and watch the sunburnt noon smite to a
finer gold the tower's gilded vanes, or wander up the
Christ Church staircase beneath the vaulted ceiling's
shadowy fans, or pass through the sculptured gate-
way of Laud's building in the College of St. John.
Nor is it merely at Oxford, or Cambridge, that the
sense of beauty can be formed and trained and per-
fected.    All over England there is a Renaissance of
the decorative Arts.    Ugliness has had its day.
Even in the houses of the rich there is taste, and the
houses of those who are not rich have been made
gracious and comely and sweet to live in.    Caliban,
poor noisy Caliban, thinks that when he has ceased
to make mows at a thing, the thing ceases to exist.
But if he mocks no longer, it is because he has been
met with mockery, swifter and keener than his own,
and for a moment has been bitterly schooled into
that silence which should seal for ever his uncouth
distorted lips.    What has been done up to now, has
been chiefly in the clearing of the way.    It is always
more difficult to destroy than it is to create, and when
what one has to destroy is vulgarity and stupidity,
the task of destruction needs not merely courage but
also contempt.    Yet it seems to me to have been, in
a measure, done.    We have got rid of what was bad.

We have now to make what is beautiful. And though the mission of the æsthetic movement is to lure people to contemplate, not to lead them to create, yet, as the creative instinct is strong in the Celt, and it is the Celt who leads in art, there is no reason why in future years this strange Renaissance should not become almost as mighty in its way as was that new birth of Art that woke many centuries ago in the cities of Italy.

Certainly, for the cultivation of temperament, we must turn to the decorative arts: to the arts that touch us, not to the arts that teach us. Modern pictures are, no doubt, delightful to look at. At least, some of them are. But they are quite impossible to live with; they are too clever, too assertive, too intellectual. Their meaning is too obvious, and their method too clearly defined. One exhausts what they have to say in a very short time, and then they become as tedious as one's relations. I am very fond of the work of many of the Impressionist painters of Paris and London. Subtlety and distinction have not yet left the school. Some of their arrangements and harmonies serve to remind one of the unapproachable beauty of Gautier's immortal *Symphonie en Blanc Majeur*, that flawless masterpiece of colour and music which may have suggested the type as well as the titles of many of

their best pictures.    For a class that welcomes the
incompetent with sympathetic eagerness, and that
confuses the bizarre with the beautiful, and vulgarity with truth, they are extremely accomplished.
They can do etchings that have the brilliancy of
epigrams, pastels that are as fascinating as paradoxes, and as for their portraits, whatever the
commonplace may say against them, no one can
deny that they possess that unique and wonderful
charm which belongs to works of pure fiction.    But
even the Impressionists, earnest and industrious as
they are, will not do.    I like them.    Their white
keynote, with its variations in lilac, was an era in
colour.    Though the moment does not make the
man, the moment certainly makes the Impressionist, and for the moment in art, and the " moment's
monument," as Rossetti phrased it, what may not
be said?    They are suggestive also.    If they have
not opened the eyes of the blind, they have at least
given great encouragement to the short-sighted, and
while their leaders may have all the inexperience
of old age, their young men are far too wise to be
ever sensible.    Yet they will insist on treating
painting as if it were a mode of autobiography
invented for the use of the illiterate, and are always
prating to us on their coarse gritty canvases of
their unnecessary selves and their unnecessary opin-

ions, and spoiling by a vulgar over-emphasis that fine contempt of nature which is the best and only modest thing about them.   One tires, at the end, of the work of individuals whose individuality is always noisy, and generally uninteresting.   There is far more to be said in favour of that newer school at Paris, the 'Archaicistes,' as they call themselves, who, refusing to leave the artist entirely at the mercy of the weather, do not find the ideal of art in mere atmospheric effect, but seek rather for the imaginative beauty of design and the loveliness of fair colour, and rejecting the tedious realism of those who merely paint what they see, try to see something worth seeing, and to see it not merely with actual and physical vision, but with that nobler vision of the soul which is as far wider in spiritual scope as it is far more splendid in artistic purpose.   They, at any rate, work under those decorative conditions that each art requires for its perfection, and have sufficient æsthetic instinct to regret those sordid and stupid limitations of absolute modernity of form which have proved the ruin of so many of the Impressionists.   Still, the art that is frankly decorative is the art to live with.   It is, of all our visible arts, the one art that creates in us both mood and temperament.   Mere colour, unspoiled by meaning, and unallied with definite form, can speak to the soul in a thousand different ways. The harmony that resides in the delicate proportions of lines and masses becomes mirrored in the mind. The repetitions of pattern give us rest. The marvels of design stir the imagination. In the mere loveliness of the materials employed there are latent elements of culture. Nor is this all. By its deliberate rejection of Nature as the ideal of beauty, as well as of the imitative method of the ordinary painter, decorative art not merely prepares the soul for the reception of true imaginative work, but develops in it that sense of form which is the basis of creative no less than of critical achievement. For the real artist is he who proceeds, not from feeling to form, but from form to thought and passion. He does not first conceive an idea, and then say to himself, "I will put my idea into a complex metre of fourteen lines," but, realizing the beauty of the sonnet-scheme, he conceives certain modes of music and methods of rhyme, and the mere form suggests what is to fill it and make it intellectually and emotionally complete. From time to time the world cries out against some charming artistic poet, because, to use its hackneyed and silly phrase, he has "nothing to say." But if he had something to say, he would probably say it, and the result would be tedious. It is just because he has no new message, that he can do beautiful work. He gains his inspiration from form, and from form purely, as an artist should.    A real passion would ruin him.    Whatever actually occurs is spoiled for art.    All bad poetry springs from genuine feeling. To be natural is to be obvious, and to be obvious is to be inartistic.

*Ernest.* I wonder do you really believe what you say.

*Gilbert.* Why should you wonder?    It is not merely in art that the body is the soul.    In every sphere of life Form is the beginning of things. The rhythmic harmonious gestures of dancing convey, Plato tells us, both rhythm and harmony into the mind.    Forms are the food of faith, cried Newman in one of those great moments of sincerity that made us admire and know the man.    He was right, though he may not have known how terribly right he was.    The Creeds are believed, not because they are rational, but because they are repeated. Yes: Form is everything.    It is the secret of life. Find expression for a sorrow, and it will become dear to you.    Find expression for a joy, and you intensify its ecstasy.    Do you wish to love?    Use Love's Litany, and the words will create the yearning from which the world fancies that they spring. Have you a grief that corrodes your heart?    Steep yourself in the language of grief, learn its utterance from Prince Hamlet and Queen Constance, and you will find that mere expression is a mode of consolation, and that Form, which is the birth of passion, is also the death of pain. And so, to return to the sphere of Art, it is Form that creates not merely the critical temperament, but also the æsthetic instinct, that unerring instinct that reveals to one all things under their conditions of beauty. Start with the worship of form, and there is no secret in art that will not be revealed to you, and remember that in criticism, as in creation, temperament is everything, and that it is, not by the time of their production, but by the temperaments to which they appeal, that the schools of art should be historically grouped.

*Ernest.* Your theory of education is delightful. But what influence will your critic, brought up in these exquisite surroundings, possess? Do you really think that any artist is ever affected by criticism?

*Gilbert.* The influence of the critic will be the mere fact of his own existence. He will represent the flawless type. In him the culture of the century will see itself realized. You must not ask of him to have any aim other than the perfecting of himself. The demand of the intellect, as has been well said, is simply to feel itself alive. The critic may, indeed, desire to exercise influence; but, if so, he will concern himself not with the individual, but with the age, which he will seek to wake into consciousness, and to make responsive, creating in it new desires and appetites, and lending it his larger vision and his nobler moods.  The actual art of to-day will occupy him less than the art of to-morrow, far less than the art of yesterday, and as for this or that person at present toiling away, what do the industrious matter?  They do their best, no doubt, and consequently we get the worst from them.  It is always with the best intentions that the worst work is done.  And besides, my dear Ernest, when a man reaches the age of forty, or becomes a Royal Academician, or is elected a member of the Athenæum Club, or is recognized as a popular novelist, whose books are in great demand at suburban railway stations, one may have the amusement of exposing him, but one cannot have the pleasure of reforming him.  And this is, I dare say, very fortunate for him; for I have no doubt that reformation is a much more painful process than punishment—is, indeed, punishment in its most aggravated and moral form—a fact which accounts for our entire failure as a community to reclaim that interesting phenomenon who is called the confirmed criminal.

*Ernest.* But may it not be that the poet is the best judge of poetry, and the painter of painting? Each art must appeal primarily to the artist who works in it. His judgment will surely be the most valuable?

*Gilbert.* The appeal of all art is simply to the artistic temperament. Art does not address herself to the specialist. Her claim is that she is universal, and that in all her manifestations she is one. Indeed, so far from its being true that the artist is the best judge of art, a really great artist can never judge of other people's work at all, and can hardly, in fact, judge of his own. That very concentration of vision that makes a man an artist, limits by its sheer intensity his faculty of fine appreciation. The energy of creation hurries him blindly on to his own goal. The wheels of his chariot raise the dust as a cloud around him. The gods are hidden from each other. They can recognize their worshippers. That is all.

*Ernest.* You say that a great artist cannot recognize the beauty of work different from his own.

*Gilbert.* It is impossible for him to do so. Wordsworth saw in *Endymion* merely a pretty piece of Paganism, and Shelley, with his dislike of actuality, was deaf to Wordsworth's message, being repelled by its form, and Byron, that great passionate human incomplete creature, could appreciate neither the poet of the cloud nor the poet of the lake, and the wonder of Keats was hidden from him. The realism of Euripides was hateful to Sophokles. Those droppings of warm tears had no music for him. Milton, with his sense of the grand style, could not understand the method of Shakespeare, any more than could Sir Joshua the method of Gainsborough. Bad artists always admire each other's worth. They call it being large-minded and free from prejudice. But a truly great artist cannot conceive of life being shown, or beauty fashioned, under any conditions other than those that he has selected. Creation employs all its critical faculty within its own sphere. It may not use it in the sphere that belongs to others. It is exactly because a man cannot do a thing that he is the proper judge of it.

*Ernest.* Do you really mean that?

*Gilbert.* Yes, for creation limits, while contemplation widens, the vision.

*Ernest.* But what about technique? Surely each art has its separate technique?

*Gilbert.* Certainly: each art has its grammar and its materials. There is no mystery about either, and the incompetent can always be correct. But, while the laws upon which Art rests may be fixed and certain to find their true realization, they must be touched by the imagination into such beauty that they will seem an exception, each one of them.  Technique is really personality.  That is the reason why the artist cannot teach it, why the pupil cannot learn it, and why the æsthetic critic can understand it.  To the great poet, there is only one method of music—his own.  To the great painter there is only one manner of painting—that which he himself employs.  The æsthetic critic, and the æsthetic critic alone, can appreciate all forms and modes.  It is to him that Art makes her appeal.

*Ernest.*  Well, I think I have put all my questions to you.  And now I must admit—

*Gilbert.*  Ah! don't say that you agree with me. When people agree with me I always feel that I must be wrong.

*Ernest.*  In that case I certainly won't tell you whether I agree with you or not.  But I will put another question.  You have explained to me that criticism is a creative art.  What future has it?

*Gilbert.*  It is to criticism that the future belongs. The subject-matter at the disposal of creation becomes every day more limited in extent and variety. Providence and Mr. Walter Besant have exhausted the obvious.  If creation is to last at all, it can only do so on the condition of becoming far more critical than it is at present. The old roads and dusty highways have been traversed too often. Their charm has been worn away by plodding feet, and they have lost that element of novelty or surprise which is so essential for romance. He who would stir us now by fiction must either give us an entirely new background, or reveal to us the soul of man in its innermost workings. The first is for the moment being done for us by Mr. Rudyard Kipling. As one turns over the pages of his *Plain Tales from the Hills,* one feels as if one were seated under a palm-tree reading life by superb flashes of vulgarity. The bright colours of the bazaars dazzle one's eyes. The jaded, second-rate Anglo-Indians are in exquisite incongruity with their surroundings. The mere lack of style in the story-teller gives an odd journalistic realism to what he tells us. From the point of view of literature Mr. Kipling is a genius who drops his aspirates. From the point of view of life, he is a reporter who knows vulgarity better than any one has ever known it. Dickens knew its clothes and its comedy. Mr. Kipling knows its essence and its seriousness. He is our first authority on the second-rate, and has seen marvellous things through key-holes, and his backgrounds are real works of art. As for the second condition, we have had Browning, and Meredith is

with us.   But there is still much to be done in the
sphere of introspection.  People sometimes say that
fiction is getting too morbid.   As far as psychology
is concerned, it has never been morbid enough.  We
have merely touched the surface of the soul, that is
all.   In one single ivory cell of the brain there are
stored away things more marvellous and more terrible than even they have dreamed of, who, like the
author of *Le Rouge et le Noir*, have sought to track
the soul into its most secret places, and to make
life confess its dearest sins.   Still, there is a limit
even to the number of untried backgrounds, and it
is possible that a further development of the habit
of introspection may prove fatal to that creative
faculty to which it seeks to supply fresh material.  I
myself am inclined to think that creation is doomed.
It springs from too primitive, too natural an impulse.   However this may be, it is certain that the
subject-matter at the disposal of creation is always
diminishing, while the subject-matter of  criticism
increases daily.   There are always new attitudes
for the mind, and new points of view.   The duty of
imposing form upon chaos does not grow less as the
world advances.   There was never a time when
Criticism was more needed than it is now.   It is
only by its means that Humanity can become conscious of the point at which it has arrived.

Hours ago, Ernest, you asked me the use of Criticism. You might just as well have asked me the use of thought. It is Criticism, as Arnold points out, that creates the intellectual atmosphere of the age. It is Criticism, as I hope to point out myself some day, that makes the mind a fine instrument. We, in our educational system, have burdened the memory with a load of unconnected facts, and laboriously striven to impart our laboriously-acquired knowledge. We teach people how to remember, we never teach them how to grow. It has never occurred to us to try and develop in the mind a more subtle quality of apprehension and discernment. The Greeks did this, and when we come in contact with the Greek critical intellect, we cannot but be conscious that, while our subject-matter is in every respect larger and more varied than theirs, theirs is the only method by which this subject-matter can be interpreted. England has done one thing; it has invented and established Public Opinion, which is an attempt to organize the ignorance of the community, and to elevate it to the dignity of physical force. But Wisdom has always been hidden from it. Considered as an instrument of thought, the English mind is coarse and undeveloped. The only thing that can purify it is the growth of the critical instinct.

It is Criticism, again, that, by concentration, makes culture possible. It takes the cumbersome mass of creative work, and distils it into a finer essence. Who that desires to retain any sense of form could struggle through the monstrous multitudinous books that the world has produced, books in which thought stammers or ignorance brawls? The thread that is to guide us across the wearisome labyrinth is in the hands of Criticism. Nay more, where there is no record, and history is either lost or was never written, Criticism can recreate the past for us from the very smallest fragment of language or art, just as surely as the man of science can from some tiny bone, or the mere impress of a foot upon a rock, recreate for us the winged dragon or Titan lizard that once made the earth shake beneath its tread, can call Behemoth out of his cave, and make Leviathan swim once more across the startled sea. Prehistoric history be-longs to the philological and archæological critic. It is to him that the origins of things are revealed. The self-conscious deposits of an age are nearly always misleading. Through philological criticism alone we know more of the centuries of which no actual record has been preserved, than we do of the centuries that have left us their scrolls. It can do for us what can be done neither by physics nor metaphysics. It can give us the exact science of mind in the process

of becoming. It can do for us what History cannot do. It can tell us what man thought before he
learned how to write. You have asked me about
the influence of Criticism. I think I have answered
that question already; but there is this also to be
said. It is Criticism that makes us cosmopolitan.
The Manchester school tried to make men realize
the brotherhood of humanity, by pointing out the
commercial advantages of peace. It sought to degrade the wonderful world into a common market-
place for the buyer and the seller. It addressed itself
to the lowest instincts, and it failed. War followed
upon war, and the tradesman's creed did not pre-
vent France and Germany from clashing together in
blood-stained battle. There are others of our own
day who seek to appeal to mere emotional sympathies, or to the shallow dogmas of some vague system
of abstract ethics. They have their Peace Societies,
so dear to the sentimentalists, and their proposals for
unarmed International Arbitration, so popular among
those who have never read history. But mere emotional sympathy will not do. It is too variable, and
too closely connected with the passions; and a board
of arbitrators who, for the general welfare of the race,
are to be deprived of the power of putting their de-
cisions into execution, will not be of much avail.
There is only one thing worse than Injustice, and

that is Justice without her sword in her hand. When Right is not Might, it is Evil.

No: the emotions will not make us cosmopolitan, any more than the greed for gain could do so. It is only by the cultivation of the habit of intellectual criticism that we shall be able to rise superior to race prejudices. Goethe—you will not misunderstand what I say—was a German of the Germans. He loved his country—no man more so. Its people were dear to him; and he led them. Yet, when the iron hoof of Napoleon trampled upon vineyard and corn-field, his lips were silent. "How can one write songs of hatred without hating?" he said to Eckermann, "and how could I, to whom culture and barbarism are alone of importance, hate a nation which is among the most cultivated of the earth, and to which I owe so great a part of my own cultivation?" This note, sounded in the modern world by Goethe first, will become, I think, the starting point for the cosmopolitanism of the future. Criticism will annihilate race prejudices, by insisting upon the unity of the human mind in the variety of its forms. If we are tempted to make war upon another nation, we shall remember that we are seeking to destroy an element of our own culture, and possibly its most important element. As long as war is regarded as wicked, it will always have its fascination. When it is looked upon as vulgar, it will cease to be popular. The change will, of course, be slow, and people will not be conscious of it. They will not say " We will not war against France because her prose is perfect," but because the prose of France is perfect they will not hate the land. Intellectual criticism will bind Europe together in bonds far closer than those that can be forged by shopman or sentimentalist. It will give us the peace that springs from understanding.

Nor is this all. It is Criticism that, recognizing no position as final, and refusing to bind itself by the shallow shibboleths of any sect or school, creates that serene philosophic temper which loves truth for its own sake, and loves it not the less because it knows it to be unattainable. How little we have of this temper in England, and how much we need it! The English mind is always in a rage. The intellect of the race is wasted in the sordid and stupid quarrels of second-rate politicians or third-rate theologians. It was reserved for a man of science to show us the supreme example of that " sweet reasonableness" of which Arnold spoke so wisely, and, alas! to so little effect. The author of the *Origin of Species* had, at any rate, the philosophic temper. If one contemplates the ordinary pulpits and platforms of England, one can but feel the contempt of Julian, or the indifference of Montaigne. We are dominated by the fanatic, whose worst vice is his sincerity. Anything approaching to the free play of the mind is practically unknown amongst us. People cry out against the sinner, yet it is not the sinful, but the stupid, who are our shame. There is no sin except stupidity.

*Ernest.* Ah! what an antinomian you are!

*Gilbert.* The artistic critic, like the mystic, is an antinomian always. To be good, according to the vulgar standard of goodness, is obviously quite easy. It merely requires a certain amount of sordid terror, a certain lack of imaginative thought, and a certain low passion for middle-class respectability. Æsthetics are higher than ethics. They belong to a more spiritual sphere. To discern the beauty of a thing is the finest point to which we can arrive. Even a colour-sense is more important, in the development of the individual, than a sense of right and wrong. Æsthetics, in fact, are to Ethics in the sphere of conscious civilization, what, in the sphere of the external world, sexual is to natural selection. Ethics, like natural selection, make existence possible. Æsthetics, like sexual selection, make life lovely and wonderful, fill it with new forms, and give it progress, and variety and change. And when we reach the true culture that is our aim, we attain to that perfection of which the saints have dreamed, the perfection of those to whom sin is impossible, not because they make the renunciations of the ascetic, but because they can do everything they wish without hurt to the soul, and can wish for nothing that can do the soul harm, the soul being an entity so divine that it is able to transform into elements of a richer experience, or a finer suscepti- bility, or a newer mode of thought, acts or passions that with the common would be commonplace, or with the uneducated, ignoble, or with the shameful vile.   Is this dangerous?  Yes; it is dangerous—all ideas, as I told you, are so.   But the night wearies, and the light flickers in the lamp. One more thing I cannot help saying to you.   You have spoken against Criticism as being a sterile thing.   The nineteenth century is a turning point in history simply on account of the work of two men, Darwin and Renan, the one the critic of the Book of Nature, the other the critic of the books of God. Not to recognize this is to miss the meaning of one of the most important eras in the progress of the world.   Creation is always behind the age.   It is Criticism that leads us.   The Critical Spirit and the World-Spirit are one.

*Ernest.* And he who is in possession of this spirit, or whom this spirit possesses, will, I suppose, do nothing ?

*Gilbert.* Like the Persephone of whom Landor tells us, the sweet pensive Persephone around whose white feet the asphodel and amaranth are blooming, he will sit contented "in that deep, motionless quiet which mortals pity, and which the gods enjoy." He will look out upon the world and know its secret. By contact with divine things, he will become divine. His will be the perfect life, and his only.

*Ernest.* You have told me many strange things to-night, Gilbert. You have told me that it is more difficult to talk about a thing than to do it, and that to do nothing at all is the most difficult thing in the world; you have told me that all Art is immoral, and all thought dangerous; that criticism is more creative than creation, and that the highest criticism is that which reveals in the work of Art what the artist had not put there; that it is exactly because a man cannot do a thing that he is the proper judge of it; and that the true critic is unfair, insincere, and not rational. My friend, you are a dreamer.

*Gilbert.* Yes; I am a dreamer. For a dreamer is one who can only find his way by moonlight, and his punishment is that he sees the dawn before the rest of the world.

*Ernest.* His punishment?

*Gilbert.* And his reward. But see, it is dawn already. Draw back the curtains and open the

windows wide.  How cool the morning air is!  Piccadilly lies at our feet like a long riband of silver.  A
faint purple mist hangs over the Park, and the
shadows of the white houses are purple.  It is too
late to sleep.  Let us go down to Covent Garden
and look at the roses.  Come!  I am tired of
thought.

# THE TRUTH OF MASKS

## A NOTE ON ILLUSION

# THE TRUTH OF MASKS

IN many of the somewhat violent attacks that have recently been made on that splendour of mounting which now characterizes our Shakespearian revivals in England, it seems to have been tacitly assumed by the critics that Shakespeare himself was more or less indifferent to the costume of his actors, and that, could he see Mrs. Langtry's production of *Antony and Cleopatra*, he would probably say that the play, and the play only, is the thing, and that everything else is leather and prunella. While, as regards any historical accuracy in dress, Lord Lytton, in an article in the *Nineteenth Century*, has laid it down as a dogma of art that archæology is entirely out of place in the presentation of any of Shakespeare's plays, and the attempt to introduce it one of the stupidest pedantries of an age of prigs.

Lord Lytton's position I shall examine later on; but, as regards the theory that Shakespeare did not busy himself much about the costume-wardrobe of his theatre, anybody who cares to study Shakespeare's method will see that there is absolutely no dramatist of the French, English, or Athenian stage who relies so much for his illusionist effects on the dress of his actors as Shakespeare does himself.

Knowing how the artistic temperament is always fascinated by beauty of costume, he constantly introduces into his plays masques and dances, purely for the sake of the pleasure which they give the eye; and we have still his stage directions for the three great processions in *Henry the Eighth*, directions which are characterized by the most extraordinary elaborateness of detail down to the collars of S.S. and the pearls in Anne Boleyn's hair. Indeed, it would be quite easy for a modern manager to reproduce these pageants absolutely as Shakespeare had them designed; and so accurate were they that one of the Court officials of the time, writing an account of the last performance of the play at the Globe Theatre to a friend, actually complains of their realistic character, notably of the production on the stage of the Knights of the Garter in the robes and insignia of the order, as being calculated to bring ridicule on the real ceremonies; much in the same spirit in which the French Government, some time ago, prohibited that delightful actor, M. Christian, from appearing in uniform, on the plea that it was prejudicial to the glory of the army that a colonel should be caricatured. And elsewhere the gorgeousness of apparel which distinguished the English stage under Shakespeare's influence was attacked by the contemporary critics, not as a rule, however, on the grounds of the democratic tendencies of realism, but usually on those moral grounds which are always the last refuge of people who have no sense of beauty.

The point, however, which I wish to emphasize is, not that Shakespeare appreciated the value of lovely costumes in adding picturesqueness to poetry, but that he saw how important costume is as a means of producing certain dramatic effects. Many of his plays, such as *Measure for Measure*, *Twelfth Night*, *The Two Gentlemen of Verona*, *All's Well that Ends Well*, *Cymbeline*, and others, depend for their illusion on the character of the various dresses worn by the hero or the heroine; the delightful scene in *Henry the Sixth*, on the modern miracles of healing by faith, loses all its point unless Gloster is in black and scarlet; and the *dénoûment* of the *Merry Wives of Windsor* hinges on the colour of Anne Page's gown. As for the uses Shakespeare makes of disguises, the instances are almost numberless. Posthumus hides his pas-

sion under a peasant's garb, and Edgar his pride
beneath an idiot's rags; Portia wears the apparel of
a lawyer, and Rosalind is attired in all points as a
man; the cloak-bag of Pisanio changes Imogen
to the youth Fidele; Jessica flees from her father's
house in boy's dress, and Julia ties up her yellow
hair in fantastic love-knots, and dons hose and
doublet; Henry the Eighth woos his lady as a
shepherd, and Romeo his as a pilgrim; Prince Hal
and Poins appear first as footpads in buckram suits,
and then in white aprons and leather jerkins as the
waiters in a tavern; and as for Falstaff, does he not
come on as a highwayman, as an old woman, as
Herne the Hunter, and as the clothes going to the
laundry?

Nor are the examples of the employment of costume as a mode of intensifying dramatic situation
less numerous. After the slaughter of Duncan, Macbeth appears in his night-gown as if aroused from
sleep; Timon ends in rags the play he had begun
in splendour; Richard flatters the London citizens
in a suit of mean and shabby armour, and, as soon
as he has stepped in blood to the throne, marches
through the streets in crown and George and Garter; the climax of the *Tempest* is reached when
Prospero, throwing off his enchanter's robes, sends
Ariel for his hat and rapier, and reveals himself as

the great Italian Duke; the very Ghost in *Hamlet*
changes his mystical apparel to produce different
effects; and as for Juliet, a modern playwright
would probably have laid her out in her shroud,
and made the scene a scene of horror merely, but
Shakespeare arrays her in rich and gorgeous raiment, whose loveliness makes the vault " a feasting
presence full of light," turns the tomb into a bridal
chamber, and gives the cue and motive for Romeo's
speech on the triumph of Beauty over Death.

Even small details of dress, such as the colour of
a major-domo's stockings, the pattern on a wife's
handkerchief, the sleeve of a young soldier, and a
fashionable woman's bonnets, become in Shakespeare's hands points of actual dramatic importance,
and by some of them the action of the play in question is conditioned absolutely.   Many other dramatists have availed themselves of costume as a method
of expressing directly to the audience the character
of a person on his entrance, though hardly so brilliantly as Shakespeare has done in the case of the
dandy Parolles, whose dress, by the way, only an
archæologist can understand; the fun of a master
and servants exchanging coats in presence of the
audience, of shipwrecked sailors squabbling over
the division of a lot of fine clothes, and of a tinker
dressed up like a duke while he is in his cups, may

be regarded as part of that great career which
costume has always played in comedy from the
time of Aristophanes down to Mr. Gilbert; but
nobody from the mere details of apparel and
adornment has ever drawn such irony of contrast,
such immediate and tragic effect, such pity and
such pathos, as Shakespeare himself.    Armed cap-
à-pie, the dead king stalks on the battlements of
Elsinore because all is not right with Denmark;
Shylock's Jewish gaberdine is part of the stigma
under which that wounded and embittered nature
writhes; Arthur begging for his life can think of
no better plea than the handkerchief he had given
Hubert—

> Have you the heart? when your head did but ache,
> I knit my handkerchief about your brows,
> (The best I had, a princess wrought it me)
> And I did never ask it you again.

and Orlando's blood-stained napkin strikes the first
sombre note in that exquisite woodland idyll, and
shows us the depth of feeling that underlies Rosalind's fanciful wit and wilful jesting.

> Last night 'twas on my arm; I kissed it;
> I hope it be not gone to tell my lord
> That I kiss aught but he.

says Imogen, jesting on the loss of the bracelet
which was already on its way to Rome to rob her

of her husband's faith; the little Prince passing to
the Tower plays with the dagger in his uncle's
girdle; Duncan sends a ring to Lady Macbeth on
the night of his own murder, and the ring of Portia
turns the tragedy of the merchant into a wife's
comedy.    The great rebel York dies with a paper
crown on his head; Hamlet's black suit is a kind of
colour-motive in the piece, like the mourning of
Chimène in the *Cid;* and the climax of Antony's
speech is the production of Cæsar's cloak: —

> I remember
> The first time ever Cæsar put it on.
> 'Twas on a summer's evening, in his tent,
> The day he overcame the Nervii : —
> Look, in this place ran Cassius' dagger through :
> See what a rent the envious Casca made :
> Through this the well-beloved Brutus stabbed. . . .
> Kind souls, what, weep you when you but behold
> Our Cæsar's vesture wounded?

The flowers which Ophelia carries with her in
her madness are as pathetic as the violets that
blossom on a grave; the effect of Lear's wandering
on the heath is intensified beyond words by his
fantastic attire; and when Cloten, stung by the
taunt of that simile which his sister draws from her
husband's raiment, arrays himself in that husband's
very garb to work upon her the deed of shame, we
feel that there is nothing in the whole of modern

French realism, nothing even in *Thérèse Raquin*, that masterpiece of horror, which for terrible and tragic significance can compare with this strange scene in *Cymbeline*.

In the actual dialogue also some of the most vivid passages are those suggested by costume. Rosalind's

> Dost thou think, though I am caparisoned like a man, I have a doublet and hose in my disposition?

Constance's

> Grief fills the place up of my absent child,
> Stuffs out his vacant garments with his form;

and the quick sharp cry of Elizabeth—

> Ah! cut my lace asunder!

are only a few of the many examples one might quote. One of the finest effects I have ever seen on the stage was Salvini, in the last act of *Lear*, tearing the plume from Kent's cap and applying it to Cordelia's lips when he came to the line,

> This feather stirs; she lives!

Mr. Booth, whose Lear had many noble qualities of passion, plucked, I remember, some fur from his archæologically-incorrect ermine for the same business; but Salvini's was the finer effect of the two, as well as the truer. And those who saw Mr.

Irving in the last act of *Richard the Third* have
not, I am sure, forgotten how much the agony and
terror of his dream was intensified, by contrast,
through the calm and quiet that preceded it, and the
delivery of such lines as

> What, is my beaver easier than it was?
> And all my armour laid into my tent?
> Look that my staves be sound and not too heavy—

lines which had a double meaning for the audience
remembering the last words which Richard's mother
called after him as he was marching to Bosworth : —

> Therefore take with thee my most grievous curse,
> Which in the day of battle tire thee more
> Than all the complete armour that thou wear'st.

As regards the resources which Shakespeare had
at his disposal, it is to be remarked that, while he
more than once complains of the smallness of the
stage on which he has to produce big historical plays,
and of the want of scenery which obliges him to cut
out many effective open-air incidents, he always
writes as a dramatist who had at his disposal a most
elaborate theatrical wardrobe, and who could rely on
the actors taking pains about their make-up.   Even
now it is difficult to produce such a play as the *Comedy of Errors ;* and to the picturesque accident of
Miss Ellen Terry's brother resembling herself we
owed the opportunity of seeing *Twelfth Night*

adequately performed. Indeed, to put any play of
Shakespeare's on the stage, absolutely as he himself
wished it to be done, requires the services of a good
property-man, a clever wig-maker, a costumier with
a sense of colour and a knowledge of textures, a
master of the methods of making-up, a fencing-mas-
ter, a dancing-master, and an artist to personally
direct the whole production. For he is most careful
to tell us the dress and appearance of each character. " Racine abhorre la réalité," says Auguste
Vacquerie somewhere; " il ne daigne pas s'occuper
de son costume. Si l'on s'en rapportait aux indica-
tions du poète, Agamemnon serait vêtu d'un sceptre
et Achille d'une épée." But with Shakespeare it is
very different. He gives us directions about the costumes of Perdita, Florizel, Autolycus, the witches in
*Macbeth*, and the apothecary in *Romeo and Juliet*,
several elaborate descriptions of his fat knight, and
a detailed account of the extraordinary garb in which
Petruchio is to be married. Rosalind, he tells us, is
tall, and is to carry a spear and a little dagger; Celia
is smaller, and is to paint her face brown so as to look
sunburnt. The children who play at fairies in Windsor Forest are to be dressed in white and green—a
compliment, by the way, to Queen Elizabeth, whose
favourite colours they were—and in white, with green
garlands and green vizors, the angels are to come to

Katherine in Kimbolton. Bottom is in homespun,
Lysander is distinguished from Oberon by his wearing an Athenian dress, and Launce has holes in his
boots. The Duchess of Gloucester stands in a white
sheet with her husband in mourning beside her. The
motley of the Fool, the scarlet of the Cardinal, and
the French lilies broidered on the English coats,
are all made occasion for jest or taunt in the dialogue.
We know the patterns on the Dauphin's armour and
the Pucelle's sword, the crest on Warwick's helmet
and the colour of Bardolph's nose. Portia has golden
hair, Phœbe is black-haired, Orlando has chestnut
curls, and Sir Andrew Aguecheek's hair hangs like
flax on a distaff, and won't curl at all. Some of the
characters are stout, some lean, some straight, some
hunchbacked, some fair, some dark, and some are to
blacken their faces. Lear has a white beard, Hamlet's father a grizzled, and Benedict is to shave his
in the course of the play. Indeed, on the subject of
stage beards Shakespeare is quite elaborate; tells
us of the many different colours in use, and gives a
hint to actors to always see that their own are prop-
erly tied on. There is a dance of reapers in rye-
straw hats, and of rustics in hairy coats like satyrs;
a masque of Amazons, a masque of Russians, and a
classical masque; several immortal scenes over a
weaver in an ass's head, a riot over the colour of a

coat which it takes the Lord Mayor of London to quell, and a scene between an infuriated husband and his wife's milliner about the slashing of a sleeve.

As for the metaphors Shakespeare draws from dress, and the aphorisms he makes on it, his hits at the costume of his age, particularly at the ridiculous size of the ladies' bonnets, and the many descriptions of the 'mundus muliebris,' from the song of Autolycus in the *Winter's Tale* down to the account of the Duchess of Milan's gown in *Much Ado About Nothing*, they are far too numerous to quote; though it may be worth while to remind people that the whole of the Philosophy of Clothes is to be found in Lear's scene with Edgar—a passage which has the advantage of brevity and style over the grotesque wisdom and somewhat mouthing metaphysics of *Sartor Resartus*. But I think that from what I have already said it is quite clear that Shakespeare was very much interested in costume. I do not mean in that shallow sense by which it has been concluded from his knowledge of deeds and daffodils that he was the Blackstone and Paxton of the Elizabethan age; but that he saw that costume could be made at once impressive of a certain effect on the audience and expressive of certain types of character and is one of the essential factors of the

means which a true illusionist has at his disposal.
Indeed to him the deformed figure of Richard was
of as much value as Juliet's loveliness; he sets the
serge of the radical beside the silks of the lord, and
sees the stage effects to be got from each; he has
as much delight in Caliban as he has in Ariel, in
rags as he has in cloth of gold, and recognizes the
artistic beauty of ugliness.

The difficulty Ducis felt about translating *Othello*
in consequence of the importance given to such a
vulgar thing as a handkerchief, and his attempt to
soften its grossness by making the Moor reiterate
" Le bandeau! le bandeau!" may be taken as an
example of the difference between ' la tragédie
philosophique ' and the drama of real life; and
the introduction for the first time of the word
' mouchoir ' at the Théâtre Français was an era in
that romantic-realistic movement of which Hugo is
the father and M. Zola the ' enfant terrible,' just
as the classicism of the earlier part of the century
was emphasized by Talma's refusal to play Greek
heroes any longer in a powdered periwig—one of
the many instances, by the way, of that desire for
archæological accuracy in dress which has distinguished the great actors of our age.

In criticising the importance given to money in
*La Comédie Humaine*, Théophile Gautier says that

Balzac may claim to have invented a new hero in
fiction, 'le héros métallique.' Of Shakespeare it
may be said that he was the first to see the dramatic
value of doublets, and that a climax may depend on
a crinoline.

The burning of the Globe Theatre—an event due,
by the way, to the results of the passion for illusion
that distinguished Shakespeare's stage-management
—has unfortunately robbed us of many important
documents; but in the inventory, still in existence,
of the costume-wardrobe of a London theatre in
Shakespeare's time, there are mentioned particular
costumes for cardinals, shepherds, kings, clowns,
friars and fools; green coats for Robin Hood's men,
and a green gown for Maid Marian; a white and
gold doublet for Henry the Fifth, and a robe for
Longshanks; besides surplices, copes, damask gowns,
gowns of cloth of gold and of cloth of silver, taffeta
gowns, calico gowns, velvet coats, satin coats, frieze
coats, jerkins of yellow leather and of black leather,
red suits, grey suits, French Pierrot suits, a robe
" for to goo invisibell," which seems inexpensive at
3*l.* 10*s.*, and four incomparable fardingales—all of
which show a desire to give every character an
appropriate dress. There are also entries of Spanish,
Moorish and Danish costumes, of helmets, lances,
painted shields, imperial crowns, and papal tiaras,

as well as of costumes for Turkish Janissaries, Roman Senators, and all the gods and goddesses of Olympus, which evidence a good deal of archæological research on the part of the manager of the theatre. It is true that there is a mention of a bodice for Eve, but probably the 'donnée' of the play was after the Fall.

Indeed, anybody who cares to examine the age of Shakespeare will see that archæology was one of its special characteristics. After that revival of the classical forms of architecture which was one of the notes of the Renaissance, and the printing at Venice and elsewhere of the masterpieces of Greek and Latin literature, had come naturally an interest in the ornamentation and costume of the antique world. Nor was it for the learning that they could acquire, but rather for the loveliness that they might create, that the artists studied these things. The curious objects that were being constantly brought to light by excavations were not left to moulder in a museum, for the contemplation of a callous curator, and the 'ennui' of a policeman bored by the absence of crime. They were used as motives for the production of a new art, which was to be not beautiful merely, but also strange.

Infessura tells us that in 1485 some workmen digging on the Appian Way came across an old Roman

sarcophagus inscribed with the name " Julia, daughter of Claudius." On opening the coffer they found
within its marble womb the body of a beautiful girl
of about fifteen years of age, preserved by the em-
balmer's skill from corruption and the decay of time.
Her eyes were half open, her hair rippled round her
in crisp curling gold, and from her lips and cheek
the bloom of maidenhood had not yet departed.
Borne back to the Capitol, she became at once the
centre of a new cult, and from all parts of the city
crowded pilgrims to worship at the wonderful shrine
till the Pope, fearing lest those who had found the
secret of beauty in a Pagan tomb might forget what
secrets Judæa's rough and rock-hewn sepulchre contained, had the body conveyed away by night, and in
secret buried. Legend though it may be, yet the
story is none the less valuable as showing us the attitude of the Renaissance towards the antique world.
Archæology to them was not a mere science for the
antiquarian; it was a means by which they could
touch the dry dust of antiquity into the very breath
and beauty of life, and fill with the new wine of
romanticism forms that else had been old and out-
worn. From the pulpit of Niccola Pisano down to
Mantegna's " Triumph of Cæsar," and the service
Cellini designed for King Francis, the influence of
this spirit can be traced; nor was it confined merely

to the immobile arts—the arts of arrested movement
—but its influence was to be seen also in the great
Græco-Roman masques which were the constant
amusement of the gay courts of the time, and in
the public pomps and processions with which the
citizens of big commercial towns were wont to greet
the princes that chanced to visit them; pageants, by
the way, which were considered so important that
large prints were made of them and published—a
fact which is a proof of the general interest at the
time in matters of such kind.

And this use of archæology in shows, so far from
being a bit of priggish pedantry, is in every way legit-
imate and beautiful. For the stage is not merely the
meeting place of all the arts, but it is also the return
of art to life. Sometimes in an archæological novel
the use of strange and obsolete terms seems to hide
the reality beneath the learning, and I dare say that
many of the readers of *Notre Dame de Paris* have
been much puzzled over the meaning of such expressions as 'la casaque à mahoitres,' 'les voulgiers,' 'le
gallimard taché d'encre,' 'les craaquiniers,' and the
like; but with the stage how different it is! The ancient world wakes from its sleep, and history moves as
a pageant before our eyes, without obliging us to have
recourse to a dictionary or an encyclopedia for the
perfection of our enjoyment. Indeed, there is not

the slightest necessity that the public should know
the authorities for the mounting of any piece.   From
such materials, for instance, as the disk of Theodo-
sius, materials with which the majority of people are
probably not very familiar, Mr. E. W. Godwin, one of
the most artistic spirits of this century in England,
created the marvellous loveliness of the first act of
*Claudian*, and showed us the life of Byzantium in
the fourth century, not by a dreary lecture and a set
of grimy casts, not by a novel which requires a glos-
sary to explain it, but by the visible presentation
before us of all the glory of that great town.   And
while the costumes were true to the smallest points of
colour and design, yet the details were not assigned
that abnormal importance which they must necessarily be given in a piecemeal lecture, but were subordinated to the rules of lofty composition and the
unity of artistic effect.   Mr. Symonds, speaking of
that great picture of Mantegna's, now in Hampton
Court, says that the artist has converted an antiquarian motive into a theme for melodies of line.   The
same could have been said with equal justice of Mr.
Godwin's scene.   Only the foolish called it pedantry,
only those who would neither look nor listen spoke
of the passion of the play being killed by its paint.
It was in reality a scene not merely perfect in its
picturesqueness, but absolutely dramatic also, get-

ting rid of any necessity for tedious descriptions, and showing us, by the colour and character of Claudian's dress, and the dress of his attendants, the whole nature and life of the man, from what school of philosophy he affected, down to what horses he backed on the turf.

And indeed archæology is only really delightful when transfused into some form of art. I have no desire to underrate the services of laborious scholars, but I feel that the use Keats made of Lemprière's Dictionary is of far more value to us than Professor Max Müller's treatment of the same mythology as a disease of language. Better *Endymion* than any theory, however sound, or, as in the present instance, unsound, of an epidemic amongst adjectives! And who does not feel that the chief glory of Piranesi's book on Vases is that it gave Keats the suggestion for his *Ode on a Grecian Urn?* Art, and art only, can make archæology beautiful; and the theatric art can use it most directly and most vividly, for it can combine in one exquisite presentation the illusion of actual life with the wonder of the unreal world. But the sixteenth century was not merely the age of Vitruvius; it was the age of Vecellio also. Every nation seems suddenly to have become interested in the dress of its neighbours. Europe began to investigate its own clothes, and the amount of books published on national costumes is quite extraordinary. At the beginning of the century the *Nuremberg Chronicle*, with its two thousand illustrations, reached its fifth edition, and before the century was over seventeen editions were published of Munster's *Cosmography*. Besides these two books there were also the works of Michael Colyns, of Hans Weigel, of Amman, and of Vecellio himself, all of them well illustrated, some of the drawings in Vecellio being probably from the hand of Titian.

Nor was it merely from books and treatises that they acquired their knowledge. The development of the habit of foreign travel, the increased commercial intercourse between countries, and the frequency of diplomatic missions, gave every nation many opportunities of studying the various forms of contemporary dress. After the departure from England, for instance, of the ambassadors from the Czar the Sultan and the Prince of Morocco, Henry the Eighth and his friends gave several masques in the strange attire of their visitors. Later on London saw, perhaps too often, the sombre splendour of the Spanish Court, and to Elizabeth came envoys from all lands, whose dress, Shakespeare tells us, had an important influence on English costume.

And the interest was not confined merely to classical dress, or the dress of foreign nations;

there was also a good deal of research, amongst
theatrical people especially, into the ancient costume of England itself: and when Shakespeare,
in the prologue to one of his plays, expresses his
regret at being unable to produce helmets of the
period, he is speaking as an Elizabethan manager
and not merely as an Elizabethan poet. At Cambridge, for instance, during his day, a play of
*Richard the Third* was performed, in which the
actors were attired in real dresses of the time, pro-
cured from the great collection of historical costume in the Tower, which was always open to the
inspection of managers, and sometimes placed at
their disposal. And I cannot help thinking that
this performance must have been far more artistic,
as regards costume, than Garrick's mounting of
Shakespeare's own play on the subject, in which he
himself appeared in a nondescript fancy dress, and
everybody else in the costume of the time of
George the Third, Richmond especially being much
admired in the uniform of a young guardsman.

For what is the use to the stage of that archæology
which has so strangely terrified the critics, but that
it, and it alone, can give us the architecture and
apparel suitable to the time in which the action of
the play passes? It enables us to see a Greek dressed
like a Greek, and an Italian like an Italian; to enjoy

the arcades of Venice and the balconies of Verona;
and, if the play deals with any of the great eras in
our country's history, to contemplate the age in its
proper attire, and the king in his habit as he lived.
And I wonder, by the way, what Lord Lytton
would have said some time ago, at the Princess's
Theatre, had the curtain risen on his father's Brutus
reclining in a Queen Anne chair, attired in a flowing
wig and a flowered dressing-gown, a costume which
in the last century was considered peculiarly appropriate to an antique Roman!   For in those halcyon
days of the drama no archæology troubled the stage,
or distressed the critics, and our inartistic grandfathers
sat peaceably in a stifling atmosphere of anachronisms, and beheld with the calm complacency of the
age of prose an Iachimo in powder and patches, a
Lear in lace ruffles, and a Lady Macbeth in a large
crinoline.   I can understand archæology being attacked on the ground of its excessive realism, but
to attack it as pedantic seems to be very much beside the mark.   However, to attack it for any reason
is foolish; one might just as well speak disrespect-
fully of the equator.   For archæology, being a science, is neither good nor bad, but a fact simply.
Its value depends entirely on how it is used, and
only an artist can use it.   We look to the archæologist for the materials, to the artist for the method.

In designing the scenery and costumes for any of Shakespeare's plays, the first thing the artist has to settle is the best date for the drama. This should be determined by the general spirit of the play, more than by any actual historical references which may occur in it. Most *Hamlets* I have seen were placed far too early. Hamlet is essentially a scholar of the Revival of Learning; and if the allusion to the recent invasion of England by the Danes puts it back to the ninth century, the use of foils brings it down much later. Once, however, that the date has been fixed, then the archæologist is to supply us with the facts which the artist is to convert into effects.

It has been said that the anachronisms in the plays themselves show us that Shakespeare was indifferent to historical accuracy, and a great deal of capital has been made out of Hector's indiscreet quotation from Aristotle. Upon the other hand, the anachronisms are really few in number, and not very important, and, had Shakespeare's attention been drawn to them by a brother artist, he would probably have corrected them. For, though they can hardly be called blemishes, they are certainly not the great beauties of his work; or, at least, if they are, their anachronistic charm cannot be emphasized unless the play is accurately mounted according to its proper date. In looking at Shakespeare's plays as

a whole, however, what is really remarkable is their
extraordinary fidelity as regards his personages and
his plots.   Many of his ' dramatis personæ ' are
people who had actually existed, and some of them
might have been seen in real life by a portion of his
audience.   Indeed the most violent attack that was
made on Shakespeare in his time was for his supposed caricature of Lord Cobham.   As for his plots,
Shakespeare constantly draws them either from au-
thentic history, or from the old ballads and traditions which served as history to the Elizabethan
public, and which even now no scientific historian
would dismiss as absolutely untrue.   And not merely
did he select fact instead of fancy as the basis of
much of his imaginative work, but he always gives
to each play the general character, the social atmosphere in a word, of the age in question.   Stupidity
he recognizes as being one of the permanent characteristics of all European civilizations ; so he sees no
difference between a London mob of his own day
and a Roman mob of Pagan days, between a silly
watchman in Messina and a silly Justice of the Peace
in Windsor.   But when he deals with higher characters, with those exceptions of each age which are so
fine that they become its types, he gives them absolutely the stamp and seal of their time.   Virgilia is
one of those Roman wives on whose tomb was

written " Domi mansit, lanam fecit," as surely as Juliet is the romantic girl of the Renaissance. He is even true to the characteristics of race. Hamlet has all the imagination and irresolution of the Northern nations, and the Princess Katharine is as entirely French as the heroine of *Divorçons*. Harry the Fifth is a pure Englishman, and Othello a true Moor.

Again when Shakespeare treats of the history of England from the fourteenth to the sixteenth centuries, it is wonderful how careful he is to have his facts perfectly right—indeed he follows Holinshed with curious fidelity. The incessant wars between France and England are described with extraordinary accuracy down to the names of the besieged towns, the ports of landing and embarkation, the sites and dates of the battles, the titles of the commanders on each side, and the lists of the killed and wounded. And as regards the Civil Wars of the Roses we have many elaborate genealogies of the seven sons of Edward the Third; the claims of the rival Houses of York and Lancaster to the throne are discussed at length; and if the English aristocracy will not read Shakespeare as a poet, they should certainly read him as a sort of early Peerage. There is hardly a single title in the Upper House, with the exception of course of the

uninteresting titles assumed by the law lords, which
does not appear in Shakespeare along with many
details of family history, creditable and discreditable.
Indeed if it be really necessary that the School
Board children should know all about the Wars of
the Roses, they could learn their lessons just as
well out of Shakespeare as out of shilling primers,
and learn them, I need not say, far more pleasur-
ably.   Even in Shakespeare's own day this use of
his plays was recognized.   " The historical plays
teach history to those who cannot read it in the
chronicles," says Heywood in a tract about the
stage, and yet I am sure that sixteenth-century
chronicles were much more delightful reading than
nineteenth-century primers are.

Of course the æsthetic value of Shakespeare's
plays does not, in the slightest degree, depend on
their facts, but on their Truth, and Truth is independent of facts always, inventing or selecting them
at pleasure.   But still Shakespeare's use of facts is
a most interesting part of his method of work, and
shows us his attitude towards the stage, and his relations to the great art of illusion.   Indeed he
would have been very much surprised at anyone
classing his plays with "fairy tales," as Lord
Lytton does; for one of his aims was to create for
England a national historical drama, which should

deal with incidents with which the public was well acquainted, and with heroes that lived in the memory of a people. Patriotism, I need hardly say, is not a necessary quality of art; but it means, for the artist the substitution of a universal for an individual feeling, and for the public the presentation of a work of art in a most attractive and popular form. It is worth noticing that Shakespeare's first and last successes were both historical plays.

It may be asked what has this to do with Shakespeare's attitude towards costume. I answer that a dramatist who laid such stress on historical accuracy of fact would have welcomed historical accuracy of costume as a most important adjunct to his illusionist method. And I have no hesitation in saying that he did so. The reference to helmets of the period in the prologue to *Henry the Fifth* may be considered fanciful, though Shakespeare must have often seen

The very casque
That did affright the air at Agincourt,

where it still hangs in the dusky gloom of Westminster Abbey, along with the saddle of that " imp of fame," and the dinted shield with its torn blue velvet lining and its tarnished lilies of gold; but the use of military tabards in *Henry the Sixth* is a bit of pure archæology, as they were not worn in the

sixteenth century; and the King's own tabard, I
may mention, was still suspended over his tomb in
St. George's Chapel, Windsor, in Shakespeare's
day. For, up to the time of the unfortunate
triumph of the Philistines in 1645, the chapels and
cathedrals of England were the great national
museums of archæology, and in them was kept the
armour and attire of the heroes of English history.
A good deal was of course preserved in the Tower,
and even in Elizabeth's day tourists were brought
there to see such curious relics of the past as
Charles Brandon's huge lance, which is still, I believe, the admiration of our country visitors; but
the cathedrals and churches were, as a rule, selected
as the most suitable shrines for the reception of the
historic antiquities. Canterbury can still show us
the helm of the Black Prince; Westminster the
robes of our kings, and in old St. Paul's the very
banner that had waved on Bosworth field was hung
up by Richmond himself.

In fact, everywhere that Shakespeare turned in
London, he saw the apparel and appurtenances of
past ages, and it is impossible to doubt that he
made use of his opportunities. The employment
of lance and shield, for instance, in actual warfare,
which is so frequent in his plays, is drawn from
archæology, and not from the military accoutre-

ments of his day; and his general use of armour in battle was not a characteristic of his age, a time when it was rapidly disappearing before firearms. Again, the crest on Warwick's helmet, of which such a point is made in *Henry the Sixth*, is absolutely correct in a fifteenth-century play when crests were generally worn, but would not have been so in a play of Shakespeare's own time, when feathers and plumes had taken their place — a fashion which, as he tells us in *Henry the Eighth*, was borrowed from France. For the historical plays, then, we may be sure that archæology was employed, and as for the others I feel certain it was the case also. The appearance of Jupiter on his eagle, thunderbolt in hand, of Juno with her peacocks, and of Iris with her many-coloured bow; the Amazon masque and the masque of the Five Worthies, may all be regarded as archæological; and the vision which Posthumus sees in prison of Sicilius Leonatus—" an old man, attired like a warrior, leading an ancient matron "—is clearly so. Of the " Athenian dress " by which Lysander is distinguished from Oberon I have already spoken; but one of the most marked instances is in the case of the dress of Coriolanus, for which Shakespeare goes directly to Plutarch. That historian, in his Life of the great Roman, tells us of the oak-wreath with which Caius Marcius was crowned, and of the curious kind of dress in which, according to ancient fashion, he had to canvass his electors; and on both of these points he enters into long disquisitions, investigating the origin and meaning of the old customs. Shakespeare, in the spirit of the true artist, accepts the facts of the antiquarian and con- verts them into dramatic and picturesque effects; indeed the gown of humility, the " woolvish gown," as Shakespeare calls it, is the central note of the play. There are other cases I might quote, but this one is quite sufficient for my purpose; and it is evident from it at any rate that, in mounting a play in the accurate costume of the time, according to the best authorities, we are carrying out Shake- speare's own wishes and method.

Even if it were not so, there is no more reason that we should continue any imperfections which may be supposed |to have characterized Shake- speare's stage-mounting than that we should have Juliet played by a young man, or give up the ad- vantage of changeable scenery. A great work of dramatic art should not merely be made expressive of modern passion by means of the actor, but should be presented to us in the form most suitable to the modern spirit. Racine produced his Roman plays in Louis-Quatorze dress on a stage crowded with spectators; but we require different conditions for the enjoyment of his art. Perfect accuracy of detail, for the sake of perfect illusion, is necessary for us. What we have to see is that the details are not allowed to usurp the principal place. They must be subordinate always to the general motive of the play. But subordination in art does not mean disregard of truth; it means conversion of fact into effect, and the assigning to each detail its proper relative value.

Les petits détails d'histoire et de vie domestique (says Hugo) doivent être scrupuleusement étudiés et reproduits par le poète, mais uniquement comme des moyens d'accroître la réalité de l'ensemble, et de faire pénétrer jusque dans les coins les plus obscurs de l'œuvre cette vie générale et puissante au milieu de laquelle les personnages sont plus vrais, et les catastrophes, par conséquent, plus poignantes. Tout doit être subordonné à ce but. L'Homme sur le premier plan, le reste au fond.

The passage is interesting as coming from the first great French dramatist who employed archæology on the stage, and whose plays, though absolutely correct in detail, are known to all for their passion, not for their pedantry—for their life, not for their learning. It is true that he has made certain concessions in the case of the employment of curious or strange expressions. Ruy Blas talks of M. de Priego as "sujet du roi" instead of "noble du roi," and An-

gelo Malipieri speaks of "la croix rouge" instead of
"la croix de gueules." But they are concessions
made to the public, or rather to a section of it.
"J'en offre ici toute mes excuses aux spectateurs
intelligents," he says in a note to one of the plays;
"espérons qu'un jour un seigneur vénitien pourra
dire tout bonnement sans péril son blason sur
le théâtre. C'est un progrès qui viendra." And,
though the description of the crest is not couched in
accurate language, still the crest itself was accurately
right. It may, of course, be said that the public do
not notice these things; upon the other hand, it
should be remembered that Art has no other aim
but her own perfection, and proceeds simply by her
own laws, and that the play which Hamlet describes
as being caviare to the general is a play he highly
praises. Besides, in England, at any rate, the public
have undergone a transformation; there is far more
appreciation of beauty now than there was a few years
ago; and though they may not be familiar with the
authorities and archæological data for what is shown
to them, still they enjoy whatever loveliness they
look at. And this is the important thing. Better
to take pleasure in a rose than to put its root under
a microscope. Archæological accuracy is merely
a condition of illusionist stage effect; it is not its
quality. And Lord Lytton's proposal that the

dresses should merely be beautiful without being
accurate is founded on a misapprehension of the nature of costume, and of its value on the stage.  This
value is twofold, picturesque and dramatic; the former depends on the colour of the dress, the latter on
its design and character.   But so interwoven are the
two that, whenever in our own day historical accuracy has been disregarded, and the various dresses
in a play taken from different ages, the result has
been that the stage has been turned into that chaos
of costume, that caricature of the centuries, the
Fancy Dress Ball, to the entire ruin of all dramatic
and picturesque effect.   For the dresses of one age
do not artistically harmonize with the dresses of another; and, as far as dramatic value goes, to confuse
the costumes is to confuse the play.   Costume is a
growth, an evolution, and a most important, perhaps
the most important, sign of the manners, customs,
and mode of life of each century.   The Puritan dislike of colour, adornment, and grace in apparel was
part of the great revolt of the middle classes against
Beauty in the seventeenth century.  A historian
who disregarded it would give us a most inaccurate
picture of the time, and a dramatist who did not avail
himself of it would miss a most vital element in producing an illusionist effect.   The effeminacy of dress
that characterized the reign of Richard the Second

was a constant theme of contemporary authors.
Shakespeare, writing two hundred years after, makes
the King's fondness for gay apparel and foreign
fashions a point in the play, from John of Gaunt's
reproaches down to Richard's own speech in the
third act on his deposition from the throne. And
that Shakespeare examined Richard's tomb in Westminster Abbey seems to me certain from York's
speech : —

> See, see, King Richard doth himself appear,
> As doth the blushing discontented sun
> From out the fiery portal of the east,
> When he perceives the envious clouds are bent
> To dim his glory.

For we can still discern on the King's robe his
favourite badge—the sun issuing from a cloud. In
fact, in every age the social conditions are so ex-
emplified in costume, that to produce a sixteenth-
century play in fourteenth-century attire, or *vice
versa*, would make the performance seem unreal
because untrue. And, valuable as beauty of effect
on the stage is, the highest beauty is not merely
comparable with absolute accuracy of detail, but
really dependent on it. To invent an entirely new
costume is almost impossible except in burlesque or
extravaganza, and as for combining the dress of
different centuries into one, the experiment would

be dangerous, and Shakespeare's opinion of the
artistic value of such a medley may be gathered
from his incessant satire of the Elizabethan dandies
for imagining that they were well dressed because
they got their doublets in Italy, their hats in Germany, and their hose in France.   And it should be
noted that the most lovely scenes that have been
produced on our stage have been those that have
been characterized by perfect accuracy, such as Mr.
and Mrs. Bancroft's eighteenth century revivals at
the Haymarket, Mr. Irving's superb production of
*Much Ado About Nothing*, and Mr. Barrett's *Claudian.*   Besides, and this is perhaps the most complete answer to Lord Lytton's theory, it must be
remembered that neither in costume nor in dialogue
is beauty the dramatist's primary aid at all.   The
true dramatist aims first at what is characteristic,
and no more desires that all his personages should
be beautifully attired than he desires that they
should all have beautiful natures or speak beautiful
English.   The true dramatist, in fact, shows us life
under the conditions of art, not art in the form of life.
The Greek dress was the loveliest dress the world
has ever seen, and the English dress of the last
century one of the most monstrous; yet we cannot
costume a play by Sheridan as we would costume
a play by Sophokles.   For, as Polonius says in his

excellent lecture—a lecture to which I am glad to have the opportunity of expressing my obligations— one of the first qualities of apparel is its expressiveness. And the affected style of dress in the last century was the natural characteristic of a society of affected manners and affected conversation—a characteristic which the realistic dramatist will highly value down to the smallest detail of accuracy, and the materials for which he can only get from archæology.

But it is not enough that a dress should be accurate; it must be also appropriate to the stature and appearance of the actor, and to his supposed condition, as well as to his necessary action in the play. In Mr. Hare's production of *As You Like It* at the St. James's Theatre, for instance, the whole point of Orlando's complaint that he is brought up like a peasant, and not like a gentleman, was spoiled by the gorgeousness of his dress, and the splendid apparel worn by the banished Duke and his friends was quite out of place. Mr. Lewis Wingfield's explanation that the sumptuary laws of the period necessitated their doing so, is, I am afraid, hardly sufficient. Outlaws, lurking in a forest and living by the chase, are not very likely to care much about ordinances of dress. They were probably attired like Robin Hood's men, to whom, indeed, they are compared in the course of the play.

And that their dress was not that of wealthy noble-
men may be seen by Orlando's words when he breaks
in upon them.   He mistakes them for robbers, and
is amazed to find that they answer him in courteous
and gentle terms.   Lady Archibald Campbell's production, under Mr. E. W. Godwin's direction, of
the same play in Coombe Wood was, as regards
mounting, far more artistic.   At least, it seemed so
to me.   The Duke and his companions were dressed
in serge tunics, leathern jerkins, high boots and
gauntlets, and wore bycocket hats and hoods.   And
as they were playing in a real forest, they found, I am
sure, their dresses extremely convenient.   To every
character in the play was given a perfectly appropriate attire, and the brown and green of their costumes harmonized exquisitely with the ferns through
which they wandered, the trees beneath which they
lay, and the lovely English landscape that sur-
rounded the Pastoral Players.   The perfect natural-
ness of the scene was due to the absolute accuracy
and appropriateness of everything that was worn.
Nor could archæology have been put to a severer
test, or come out of it more triumphantly.   The
whole production showed once for all that, unless a
dress is archælogically correct, and artistically appropriate, it always looks unreal, unnatural, and
theatrical in the sense of artificial.

Nor, again, is it enough that there should be accurate and appropriate costumes of beautiful colours; there must be also beauty of colour on the stage as a whole, and as long as the background is painted by one artist, and the foreground figures independently designed by another, there is the danger of a want of harmony in the scene as a picture. For each scene the colour-scheme should be settled as absolutely as for the decoration of a room, and the textures which it is proposed to use should be mixed and re-mixed in every possible combination, and what is discordant removed. Then, as regards the particular kinds of colours, the stage is often made too glaring, partly through the excessive use of hot, violent reds, and partly through the costumes looking too new. Shabbiness, which in modern life is merely the tendency of the lower orders towards tone, is not without its artistic value, and modern colours are often much improved by being a little faded. Blue also is too frequently used: it is not merely a dangerous colour to wear by gaslight, but it is really difficult in England to get a thoroughly good blue. The fine Chinese blue, which we all so much admire, takes two years to dye, and the English public will not wait so long for a colour. Peacock blue, of course, has been employed on the stage, notably at the Lyceum,

with great advantage; but all attempts at a good
light blue, or good dark blue, which I have seen
have been failures. The value of black is hardly
appreciated; it was used effectively by Mr. Irving in
*Hamlet* as the central note of a composition, but as
a tone-giving neutral its importance is not recognized. And this is curious, considering the general
colour of the dress of a century in which, as Baudelaire says, "Nous célébrons tous quelque enterre-
ment." The archæologist of the future will probably point to this age as a time when the beauty of
black was understood; but I hardly think that, as
regards stage-mounting or house decoration, it really
is. Its decorative value is, of course, the same as
that of white or gold; it can separate and har-
monise colours. In modern plays the black frock
coat of the hero becomes important in itself, and
should be given a suitable background. But it
rarely is. Indeed the only good background for a
play in modern dress which I have ever seen was
the dark grey and cream-white scene of the first
act of the *Princesse Georges* in Mrs. Langtry's production. As a rule, the hero is smothered in ' bric-
à-brac' and palm trees, lost in the gilded abyss of
Louis Quatorze furniture, or reduced to a mere
midge in the midst of marqueterie; whereas the
background should always be kept as a background,

and colour subordinated to effect.   This, of course, can only be done when there is one single mind directing the whole production.   The facts of art are diverse, but the essence of artistic effect is unity. Monarchy, Anarchy, and Republicanism may contend for the government of nations; but a theatre should be in the power of a cultured despot.   There may be division of labour, but there must be no division of mind.   Whoever understands the costume of an age understands of necessity its architecture and its surroundings also, and it is easy to see from the chairs of a century whether it was a century of crinolines or not.   In fact, in art there is no specialism, and a really artistic production should bear the impress of one master, and one master only, who not merely should design and arrange everything, but should have complete control over the way in which each dress is to be worn.

Mademoiselle Mars, in the first production of *Hernani*, absolutely refused to call her lover " Mon Lion !" unless she was allowed to wear a little fashionable toque then much in vogue on the Boulevards; and many young ladies on our own stage insist to the present day on wearing stiff starched petticoats under Greek dresses, to the entire ruin of all delicacy of line and fold; but these wicked things should not be allowed.   And there should be far more dress rehearsals than there are now. Actors such as Mr. Forbes-Robertson, Mr. Conway, Mr. George Alexander, and others, not to mention older artists, can move with ease and elegance in the attire of any century; but there are not a few who seem dreadfully embarrassed about their hands if they have no side pockets, and who always wear their dresses as if they were costumes. Costumes, of course, they are to the designer; but dresses they should be to those that wear them. And it is time that a stop should be put to the idea, very prevalent on the stage, that the Greeks and Romans always went about bareheaded in the open air—a mistake the Elizabethan managers did not fall into, for they gave hoods as well as gowns to their Roman senators.

More dress rehearsals would also be of value in explaining to the actors that there is a form of gesture and movement that is not merely appropriate to each style of dress, but really conditioned by it. The extravagant use of the arms in the eighteenth century, for instance, was the necessary result of the large hoop, and the solemn dignity of Burleigh owed as much to his ruff as to his reason. Besides, until an actor is at home in his dress, he is not at home in his part.

Of the value of beautiful costume in creating an

artistic temperament in the audience, and producing
that joy in beauty for beauty's sake without which
the great masterpieces of art can never be understood, I will not here speak; though it is worth
while to notice how Shakespeare appreciated that
side of the question in the production of his
tragedies, acting them always by artificial light, and
in a theatre hung with black; but what I have tried
to point out is that archæology is not a pedantic
method, but a method of artistic illusion, and that
costume is a means of displaying character without
description, and of producing dramatic situations
and dramatic effects.  And I think it is a pity that
so many critics should have set themselves to attack one of the most important movements on the
modern stage before that movement has at all
reached its proper perfection.  That it will do
so, however, I feel as certain as that we shall require from our dramatic critics in the future
higher qualifications than that they can remember
Macready or have seen Benjamin Webster; we
shall require of them, indeed, that they cultivate a
sense of beauty.  " Pour être plus difficile, la tâche
n'en est que plus glorieuse."  And if they will not
encourage, at least they must not oppose, a movement of which Shakespeare of all dramatists would
have most approved, for it has the illusion of truth

for its method, and the illusion of beauty for its result. Not that I agree with everything that I have said in this essay. There is much with which I entirely disagree. The essay simply represents an artistic standpoint, and in æsthetic criticism attitude is everything. For in art there is no such thing as a universal truth. A Truth in art is that whose contradictory is also true. And just as it is only in art-criticism, and through it, that we can apprehend the Platonic theory of ideas, so it is only in art-criticism, and through it, that we can realize Hegel's system of contraries. The truths of metaphysics are the truths of masks.